T. E. Lawrence:

a reader's guide

T. E. Lawrence:
a reader's guide

Frank Clements

Archon Books
1973

Library of Congress Cataloging in Publication Data

Clements, Frank.
  T. E. Lawrence: a reader's guide.

  1. Lawrence, Thomas Edward, 1888–1935—Bibliography.
Z8491.5.C57   016.828'9'1208   72–8438
ISBN 0–208–01313–X

COPYRIGHT NOTICE
© Frank Clements 1972

First published 1972 by David & Charles (Holdings) Limited, Newton Abbot, Devon, and in 1973 in the United States of America as an Archon Book by The Shoe String Press, Inc., Hamden, Connecticut 06514

Printed in Great Britain

Contents

Author's Note

The controversy surrounding T. E. Lawrence has continued un-abated throughout the years and shows no signs of ceasing. Almost every book or periodical article exhibits some degree of either adulation or hostility. This list of works by and about him takes no standpoint and represents expressions of opinion from one extreme to another.

In company with others, as the mass of material on Lawrence indicates, I have been fascinated by the man and his motives and this work is a tangible expression of this interest. Any observa-tions made regarding particular items are personal, based on a reading of the text, and are an attempt to provide a guide to the reader, not a complete critical appraisal. It has been my aim to examine every item listed in this work but this has not always proved possible, especially with regard to material of Arabic origin and some rare items housed in American libraries and private collections.

A work of this nature always owes a great deal to other people, especially the staff of public libraries responsible for the inter-library loans system. In particular I would like to thank the staffs of Birmingham, Westminster, Dorset and Plymouth Public Libraries, and the bibliographical departments of the British Museum and the Library of Congress. My special thanks are due to Madam Sama el Mahassini of the Zahiriah National Library in Damascus, and to Allan Chapman, who first inspired me with the idea of attempting this work.

Arrangement

After the Introduction, this book is arranged in sections, beginning with works by T. E. Lawrence and ending with items of a miscellaneous nature. The arrangement of each section is alphabetical by author or title, but minor variations may be indicated at the beginning of the relevant section.

Bibliographical descriptions have been given for important items but those of a general nature, with limited references to Lawrence, have just been given a standard catalogue entry to identify them. In general works containing substantial references to Lawrence, the page numbers have been given except where these are too numerous to list individually. The entries covering works of Arabic origin are, with one exception, based on information supplied by the Zahiriah National Library in Damascus, and it was not possible to obtain fuller descriptions.

A few brief notes have been given in the form of an appendix concerning the writing and publishing of *The Seven Pillars of Wisdom* and *Revolt in the Desert*. This information is based on Lawrence's own account of the writing of the two works.

TERMS USED IN THE TEXT

AMS   Autographed manuscript
App   Appendix
Bibl   Bibliography
Frontis Frontispiece
Illus   Illustrations

Arrangement

Jnl	Journal
L	Leaf
Mo	Follows a numeral and indicates the number of pages made by folding a sheet of paper
MS	Manuscript
nd	No date
np	No pagination
OLs	Oversize leaves
p (pp)	Page (pages)
Qtly	Quarterly
recto	Right-hand page
refs	References
signatures	Symbols at the bottom of each gathering to indicate the order of binding
trs	Translator
verso	Left-hand page, reverse of the recto
vol	Volume

Introduction

In any consideration of Lawrence the most striking characteristic to emerge is the complexity of the man, not only as an individual but in the effect he had on others. Was he the charlatan as perceived by Richard Aldington, or the prophet described by Eric Kennington as one who 'has lived with us in the flesh, as one of us, and, dying, has left us quickened by his spiritual message'? The truth probably lies somewhere in between, but the difficulty of ascertaining it is in part due to Lawrence, who in the words of Robert Graves, 'fought coherence. I could not, and cannot, do for him what he had set his face against doing for himself.'

This lack of coherence is the fascination that is Lawrence; his complexities provide the material for the interest he arouses. The further one delves into the legend the more there seems to be to discover about the man, with each writer exploring a different facet. It is because of this that interest in Lawrence has persisted. The legend was brought before the public through the lectures of Lowell Thomas, and its reception was in part due to the picture the desert war presented in comparison with the squalid scene in the trenches of Europe. This version of the legend persisted for some years and was only subjected to a searching examination by the appearance of Aldington's *Lawrence of Arabia* in 1955. Doubts had been expressed about certain aspects of Lawrence's account of the Arab Revolt as described in *The Seven Pillars of Wisdom* and other writings, but not until Aldington's book had the revolt and Lawrence been subjected to such a searching examination, resulting in the view that he was 'at least half a fraud'. This caused a fresh look at Lawrence, with reactions from Lawrence's defenders and from his critics.

Further interest in Lawrence came with the publication in 1968 (in the London paper *The Sunday Times*) of articles by Phillip Knightley and Colin Simpson, appearing in book form in 1969 as *The Secret Lives of Lawrence of Arabia*, and making an even closer examination of Lawrence. This study is of greater value and significance because of the use that it makes of the embargoed Lawrence papers in the Bodleian Library and of official papers not available to Aldington. It is also significant for the revelations of Bruce concerning Lawrence's mental state after the war and his masochistic tendencies. Although this work endorses part of Aldington's judgement that Lawrence was 'the appropriate hero for his class and epoch'[1] it goes even further and asserts that the whole of Lawrence's activities in the Middle East were a result of his position in British Intelligence which was far more important than one might gather from his army rank, and indeed that his work in this capacity had begun at Carchemish whilst on the British Museum dig.

In recent years Lawrence has been the subject of psychological study centred on his writings and his apparent sexual problems. Much has been made of his mental state as revealed by *The Seven Pillars*, from which writers have discerned the existence of the third 'I' who was someone existing between Lawrence the author and the Lawrence that appeared on the printed page. In this connection the articles by André Malraux, Irving Howe and John E. Mack are worthy of careful study.

Lawrence's life falls into three main parts. The first comprises his archaeological work which began with his thesis 'Crusader Castles', followed by his work at Carchemish. The second phase is that encompassed by the Arab Revolt and its immediate aftermath, beginning with his work with the Arab Bureau and concluding with his work with the Colonial Office. The last phase covers his period of service in the Air Force and Tank Corps, concluding with his death in 1935. Apart from Knightley and Simpson's claim that Lawrence's archaeological work was a cover for his intelligence activities, it is the last two phases of his life that have probably attracted the bulk of the interest and certainly the greatest controversy.

In considering each aspect of Lawrence's life there is material from his pen in the form of books or letters to balance against the material written about him, and this is especially true about the Arab Revolt. Despite its failings, *The Seven Pillars of Wisdom* remains the major work on the revolt and indeed the major literary output from Lawrence. Controversy has raged as to whether it is an accurate record of the revolt, or an account designed to show Lawrence and the Arab cause in the best light, with events so described as to stress his importance to the Arab cause, and the Arab cause presented as far more important to Allenby than in fact it was. All writers seem to agree that whatever else it might be, *The Seven Pillars* cannot be a completely accurate record because it was a conscious rewrite of events and, in the words of Liddell Hart, 'It was too conscious a pursuit of artistic achievement'. This was true as much of its physical presentation as of its content.

Much of what Lawrence wrote in *The Seven Pillars* has been countered by him in his writings elsewhere, and this is especially true of his attitude towards the ideal of the Arab cause and his feelings towards the peace settlement. Lawrence conveys the impression that he was a driving force behind the declaration of the revolt, whereas the prime mover in all the discussions was Ronald Storrs. Negotiations were well advanced before Lawrence left for Cairo and it is almost certain that the revolt would have taken place without Lawrence's presence. The question of Arab national aspirations and the policy of the allies troubled him deeply and his dilemma is shown in *The Seven Pillars*:

> I could see that if we won the war the promises to the Arabs were dead paper. Had I been an honourable adviser I would have sent my men home, and not let them risk their lives for such stuff.[2]

This deception is justified by the statement that:

> ... by leading these Arabs madly in the final victory, I would

establish them, with arms in their hands, in a position so assured (if not dominant) that expediency would counsel to the Great Powers a fair settlement of their claims.[3]

This is not compatible with his views on the Arabs expressed in a paper entitled 'The Politics of Mecca', in which he viewed any resultant independent Arab state as remaining 'in a state of political mosaic, a tissue of small jealous principalities incapable of cohesion'.[4] *The Secret Lives of Lawrence of Arabia* argues that Lawrence's only interest was to secure a British sphere of influence in the Middle East and to prevent the French gaining a foothold. Any promises that might have been made to the Arabs were to achieve this aim, and any Arab states were to remain firmly under Britain's control. This problem of conflicting interests caused Lawrence a great deal of mental stress because he was constantly playing a double game, the aim being to secure British interests in the face of Arab aspirations and French interests.

It was supposed by some writers that Lawrence's apparent failure to obtain independence for the Arabs was the reason for his joining the Air Force, but the facts do not seem to support this view: Lawrence wrote in *The Seven Pillars* that the 1921 peace settlement made with Churchill was a vindication of all his work, 'So we were quit of the war-time Eastern adventure with clean hands'. This aspect of Lawrence's life, especially the idea of Arab independence, is given a different interpretation by J. M. Wilson in his introduction to *Minorities*. He maintains that 'there is no basis for the common assumption that his early sentiments towards the Arabs and against French colonization formed part of a sustained (uncritically Francophobic) policy afterwards evident at the Peace Conference'.[5] Wilson feels that in every case Lawrence's opinion had a distinct cause, with his attitude towards the French being coloured by their practice of imposing their language and culture on their colonies, measures which would have destroyed the Arab society he revered. His attitude towards French aspirations in Syria was a result of this and his promises to Feisal, and the peace settlement was, in Wilson's view, a satisfactory conclusion for Lawrence as it gave Iraq to Feisal.

The third part of Lawrence's life, that of service in the ranks, has of course provided much food for debate, with the main reason advanced for his choosing this step being the failure of his Arabian policy. This reason is questionable in view of Lawrence's own statements on the subject, and Wilson sees no reason to dispute Lawrence's claim that he had made this decision in 1919 and that the delay was motivated by the desire to see a fair settlement of the Arab problem with the Colonial Office. In a letter to Robert Graves in August 1927 he wrote that 'these friendly outings with the armoured car and Air Force fellows were what persuaded me that my best future, if I survived the war, was to enlist'.[6] He was not at all sure himself of the real reasons for enlisting, though in part he felt that by the degradation of the transfer from being Lawrence of Arabia to being an enlisted man he might 'find myself on common ground with men . . . by an itch to make myself ordinary in a mob of likes: also I'm broke so far as money goes'.[7]

The difficulty with which Lawrence made the initial transfer is conveyed by *The Mint*, which reveals the degradation, the boredom and the crudity of the recruits' barrack-room life. After this early period there is little doubt that he began to settle into the way of life; but this was destroyed by his exposure and discharge from the service in 1922, and he found the Tank Corps to be no substitute. He did spend a great deal of time himself, and through the offices of his friends in high places, trying to arrange for his transfer back to the Air Force, but without success.

It is at this stage that one must introduce the strange story of John Bruce and his relationship with Lawrence, which began in

1920 whilst Lawrence was still with the Colonial Office. At first the relationship was normal enough, with Bruce being paid a weekly retainer to undertake various tasks for Lawrence, but the friendship was, according to Bruce, to take on a different character after Lawrence's discharge from the Air Force. Bruce, who was then only nineteen, stated that Lawrence persuaded him to join the Tank Corps with him, a move that Lawrence was taking because of pressure from the 'Old Man'. This was a creation of Lawrence's imagination; the 'Old Man' was supposed to be his uncle and to exercise control over his life, including requiring Lawrence to undergo corporal punishment. Bruce's account of the creation of an uncle, first disclosed by Knightley and Simpson in their *Sunday Times* series of articles and subsequently in *The Secret Lives of Lawrence of Arabia*, is believed by Professor Lawrence to be substantially correct. Bruce maintains that on several occasions up to 1934 he subjected Lawrence to floggings on the instructions of the 'Old Man', and on one occasion he prevented Lawrence from committing suicide at Clouds Hill. Although Bruce was recalling events of some forty-seven years earlier, the authors believe that, apart from lapses in memory and some allowance for embellishment, the story is almost certainly true.

The events described are supposed to have happened during a period when Lawrence was undergoing considerable mental strain with his struggle to get back into the Air Force and the emotional drain of writing *The Seven Pillars of Wisdom*. He achieved his ambition in 1925, the Air Force accepting him and posting him firstly to Cranwell and thence to Karachi. Trouble on the Afghanistan frontier led to newspaper stories of his involvement and his eventual recall to England. He was posted to Mount Batten, being sympathetically received by the commanding officer, Sydney Smith, and his wife, whose account of the friendship is contained in her book *The Golden Reign*.

Lawrence's time at Mount Batten seems to have been the happiest period of his life, with little of the mental recrimination of the immediate post-war years. His interest in the Schneider Cup Trophy Contest, and his work on high-speed launches, allowed use of his creative talents as did his occasional reviewing work and his friendship with the Smiths and the Shaws. His contentment was spoilt only by thoughts of impending retirement and the uncertainty of the future. What Lawrence would have achieved during his retirement and, perhaps even more interesting, during the turbulent end of the thirties can only be conjecture, because of his death in May 1935.

It is impossible to be dogmatic about any aspect of Lawrence's life and certainly the definitive biography has yet to be written. He remains a complex character, an aura of mystery and uncertainty surrounding him and his deeds. That he was a man of outstanding ability, a good soldier, with a quality for leadership and a sense of the dramatic, is beyond question. He was also a man of his time and one who attracted both devoted friendship and admiration and equally impassioned opposition. Regarding his motives in the Middle East one is drawn to the conclusion that his interests were those of Britain, and that whatever he desired for the Arabs must be subservient to that main cause.

In considering the emotional side of his character the situation is even more complex as only inferences can be drawn. There have been frequent allegations that he was a homosexual, it is a fact that he abhorred physical contact, but whether he was a homosexual is impossible to say. The incident at Deraa remains obscure, especially whether or not the Turks knew the identity of their prisoner, but it does seem that he was definitely the subject of a homosexual assault. It was also true that he pushed his body to its physical, and possibly mental, limits and this may be consistent with John Bruce's story of having satisfied Lawrence's masochistic needs. Certainly he underwent considerable mental stress, as is shown by his letters and the observations of his friends.

Lawrence's literary fame rests, in the public eye, mainly with *The Seven Pillars of Wisdom* and its abridgement, *Revolt in the Desert*. The abridgement is the more easily readable of the two as it omits the introspection of the parent work and concentrates mainly on the military campaign. It was a considerable accomplishment in itself, undertaken in three months early in 1926, and reducing the text of *The Seven Pillars* by more than half. Lawrence in fact wrote to Edward Garnett that it was 'better than the complete text. Half a calamity is better than a whole one'.[8]

The subscribers' edition of *The Seven Pillars* was aimed at being deluxe in every sense of the word: the cost of production was £13,000 for 190 copies selling at £30 each. This placed Lawrence heavily in debt and it was the need for money that led to *Revolt in the Desert*. A full account of the story behind the publishing of the two books can be found in *Jonathan Cape, Publisher* by Michael S. Howard.

On its appearance *The Seven Pillars* received mixed reviews and, as has already been said, a certain amount of criticism. One eminent critic, Sir Herbert Read, attacked both its presentation—'all that a book should not be. It is an amateur's nightmare'[9]—and its content, which he found far too difficult to read and lacking in a hero. Other writers have criticised the work because of its inaccuracies, some claiming that Lawrence manipulated the events on paper to show the Arabs and himself in the best light. One example of this type of criticism concerns Lawrence's account of the capture of Damascus, which is strongly contested by Elie Kedourie in his book *The Chatham House Version and other Middle-Eastern Studies*. Lawrence himself commented on the Damascus section of *The Seven Pillars* that 'I was on thin ice when I wrote the Damascus chapter and anyone who copies me will be through it, if he is not careful. S.P. is full of half truths here'.[10] Kedourie makes the point that the Turks had abandoned Damascus and that the Sherifian forces 'were allowed to occupy it and to claim that they had captured it',[11] and this, Kedourie claims, is substantiated by the Australian War Diaries of the Mounted Division and those of its units who participated in the campaign around Damascus. But despite its failings, *The Seven Pillars* possesses lasting qualities and is considered to be one of the most widely read books in the English language.

The Mint is Lawrence's other major work and is an account of his early days in the Air Force, though it was not published until 1955 as a result of an embargo by Lawrence which was maintained by Professor A. W. Lawrence. It appeared in two editions, one of which was expurgated to remove the barrack-room language. Once again the work was the subject of mixed reactions, some reviewers regarding it as excellent, others as a masterpiece which just failed, and others as a rank bad book. *The Mint* is certainly not as good as *The Seven Pillars*, especially from the stylistic viewpoint, though it must be remembered that it was a day-to-day notebook of life as a recruit at the Uxbridge Depot. It must also be viewed in the context of Lawrence's mental state at the time, and its true value probably lies in the insight that it gives into this period of his life and especially the difficulties involved in making the transition.

The minor writings include some of Lawrence's best work, and in particular the Diary of 1911 gives a vivid description of the Arab landscape, the people and the way in which Lawrence pushed himself to his physical limits. *The Evolution of A Revolt* is a valuable collection of these minor writings, helping to put *The Seven Pillars of Wisdom* into context by quoting the abandoned opening, and expressing Lawrence's attitude towards the post-war situation in the Middle East. His attitudes to the rivalry which existed between the India Office, the War Office and the

Foreign Office with all its attendant problems, especially with regard to Syria and Mesopotamia, are also conveyed.

Lawrence's letters are a further source of information, although he was not a letter-writer by habit and consequently they lack the standing of being considered as literary pieces in their own right. Finally we come to the only recently published collection of poems titled *Minorities*. It was a collection which Lawrence used frequently, although with many of the poems the interest rested only in a phrase, a verse or an idea. J. M. Wilson's introduction to the collection provides a useful reappraisal of Lawrence; Mr Wilson states that he considers the poems to be an important source of biographical information covering the period from the fall of Damascus to the start of *The Mint* in 1922, where no other material of a personal nature exists.

Any study of Lawrence involves one in a series of complex situations coloured by personal feelings, nationalistic fervour, politics and psychological questions. The majority of these questions have more than one answer or interpretation, and as yet the real Lawrence has escaped scrutiny—or, it would be truer to say, each writer has revealed something of the Lawrence that he personally has discovered. The position is perhaps best summed up by Margot Hill:

> He was faceted to a thousand different angles, and the particular facet one caught and called Lawrence depended on the angle at which one caught it. That, I think, is why no satisfactorily homogeneous individual emerges, as sculptors say, 'in the round', either from his own writings or the many concerning him. One can only try to describe the Lawrence one knew, without pretension that it was any more real a Lawrence than the next man's.[12]

NOTES

1   Aldington, R. *Lawrence of Arabia*, p 388
2   *The Seven Pillars of Wisdom*, Ch XLVIII
3   *Seven Pillars* (Penguin edition, Introduction)
4   PRO, FO, 414/461
5   Lawrence, T. E. *Minorities*, p 41
6   Letter to Robert Graves, August 1927 (*T. E. Lawrence to His Biographers Robert Graves and Liddell Hart*, Part 1, p 95)
7   Letter to Robert Graves, November 1922 (ibid, p 23)
8   *Letters of T. E. Lawrence*, p 284
9   Read, H. 'The Seven Pillars of Wisdom', *Bibliophile's Almanack*, 1928, p 36
10 *T. E. Lawrence to his Biographer Robert Graves*, p 104
11 Kedourie, E. *The Chatham House Version*, p 35
12 Hill, M. 'T. E. Lawrence: some trivial memories', *Virginia Quarterly Review*, October 1945, pp 598-9

Section A

Works by T. E. Lawrence, J. H. Ross and T. E. Shaw,
including contributions to periodicals

Crusader Castles, Part I, 1936

CRUSADER | CASTLES | by | T. E. LAWRENCE | THE | GOLDEN COCKEREL PRESS | 1936 | I | THE THESIS

1L + pp (1)–56 + 7Ls of plates + 1L, 25½cm.

L 1, blank; p (1), Title-page; verso, printed and published in Great Britain by Christopher Sandford, | Francis J. Newbery and Owen Rutter at the Golden Cockerel Press, | 10 Staple Inn, London, and completed on the 20 May 1936. The | edition is limited to 1,000 numbered copies printed in Perpetua type | on British mould-made paper; pp 3–5, Foreword by A. W. Lawrence; pp 6–7, Facsimile of manuscript; p 8, blank; pp 9–10, List of Contents; p 11, Explanation of the references in the notes; p 12, Map of Syria and Edessa; pp 13–(56), Text (with plates: 1–78a); 7Ls of plates; (plates: 79–96); + 1L, blank.

This work represents the thesis which gained Lawrence a First-class Honours degree in History. The scope of the thesis was defined as 'The influence of the Crusades on European Military Architecture to the end of the Twelfth Century'. It is the result of visits made by Lawrence to nearly all the important castles in England and Wales, France, Syria and Northern Palestine between 1906 and 1909.

At this early stage in his life the interest in archaeology was evident from the quality of his work which gained him the degree. Characteristic too was the manner in which he collected the material for his thesis as the information in Europe was gathered after riding across the countryside on a bicycle, and that in the Middle East on foot during the hottest part of the summer and living mainly off the land with little money and little food. After this journey it was little wonder that the countryside and the ways of the people were not unfamiliar to him. Pencilled annotations were added to the presented thesis by Lawrence, and these are reproduced in the published version.

Crusader Castles, Part II, 1936

CRUSADER | CASTLES | by | T. E. LAWRENCE | THE GOLDEN COCKEREL PRESS | 1936 | II | THE LETTERS

pp (1)–(64), 25½cm.

pp (1)–(2), blank; Frontispiece; p (3), Title-page; verso, Printed and published in Great Britain by Christopher Sandford, | Francis J. Newbery and Owen Rutter at the Golden Cockerel Press, | 10 Staple Inn, London, and completed on the 1 August 1936. The edition is limited to 1,000 copies printed in Perpetua type on British mould-made paper; pp 5–6, Preface by Mrs Lawrence; p (7), Half title; p (8), blank; pp 9–62, Text; pp (63)–(64), blank; (10Ls of plates within text; numerous sketches and diagrams throughout the text).

The letters, which Lawrence wrote to his mother whilst he was collecting material for his thesis, were never intended for publication. They were printed as a companion volume to the thesis as it was felt they would add interest to the main work.

The Diary, 1937

THE DIARY | OF T. E. | LAWRENCE MCMXI

39Ls + 13 illustrations + 4Ls (no signatures, no pagination)

3Ls, blank; L 4, Title-page; verso, blank; L 5, A NOTE CONCERNING THE | ILLUSTRATIONS; verso, blank; L 6, THE PHOTOGRAPHS AT THE END OF THE VOLUME (etc); verso, blank; L 7, A NOTE CONCERNING THE TEXT | OF THIS DIARY; verso, blank; L 8, THIS DIARY WAS KEPT (etc); verso, blank; L 9, TO T.E.L. | 18 February 1914; L 10, Half-title; Ls 11–29, Text; L 30, blank; L 31, THREE LETTERS TO MRS LAWRENCE | WRITTEN DURING THE AUTHOR'S JOURNEY IN SYRIA; verso, blank; L 32, blank; Ls 33–8, Text of Letters; 13 photographs; versos, blank; L 39, Of this Diary 203 copies have been printed, all of | which have been numbered. 150 copies only are for | sale. The type for the text is 18pt Bible Centaur. | The papers used are hand made by J. B. Green & | Son. 30 copies, Numbered 1 to 30, have been printed | on 'Canute' Paper; 40 copies, Numbered 31 to 70, have | been printed on 'Medway' Paper, and 130 copies, | Numbered 71 to 200, have been printed on Parchment | substitute paper. There are also 3 copies, Lettered A, | B, and C, Printed on Papier D'Auvergne, Green Hand- | Made Parchment paper, and Grey Japanese Paper, | which are not for sale. | This is Number | 14 | Completed at The Corvinus Press during June 1937 | Laus Deo; verso, blank; 4Ls, blank.

This trip by Lawrence was taken after the British Museum had decided to cease work at Carchemish and he made this walking tour to Horran, Urfa, Biredjik, Tell Basher and Aleppo, taking in all about one month. The journey was really concerned with his interest in the castles of the area, some of which he had visited in 1909 in connection with his thesis, and with the collection of engraved seal stones. The diary was a pencil record kept in a canvas-bound notebook and has been reprinted with only minor editing and footnotes by A. W. Lawrence. The diary is a day-to-day record of the journey, containing details of the various castles visited, the villages, his food and, above all, the people.

In his introduction, A. W. Lawrence states that he felt the

diary must have been kept by his brother with a view to eventual publication though it would probably have been rewritten. The limited edition appeared in 1937 and the diary also formed part of *Oriental Assembly* in 1939 (see p 42).

An Essay on Flecker, 1937, English Edition

AN ESSAY ON FLECKER | by | T. E. LAWRENCE

18Ls (no signature, no pagination), 30cm.

4Ls blank; L 5, Title; verso, blank; Ls 6–13, Text (rectos only, versos, blank); L 14, 30 copies of this book have been | printed on J. B. Green unsized | parchment paper. The setting of | the text is in 14pt Pastonchi | type. All copies are numbered | completed at the Corvinus Press | during the Coronation week of | King George The Sixth. | May, 1937 Laus Deo; verso, blank; Ls 15–18, blank.

An Essay on Flecker, 1937, American Edition

AN ESSAY ON FLECKER | by | T. E. LAWRENCE (device) DOUBLEDAY, DORAN AND COMPANY, INC | *Garden City, New York* | MCMXXXVII

1L + pp (1)–4 + 1L.

L 1, Title; verson, printed at the *Country Life Press*, Garden City, NY USA. Copyright 1937 | by DOUBLEDAY, DORAN AND COMPANY, INC | All Rights Reserved | First Edition; | pp (1)–4; Text; L 2, blank.

This work was issued in uncovered boards.

Evolution of a Revolt, 1968

EVOLUTION | OF   A   REVOLT | (rule) | *Early   Post-war Writings* | OF T. E. LAWRENCE | (rule) | edited with an introduction by | STANLEY and RODELLE WEINTRAUB | 1968 | THE PENNSYLVANIA STATE UNIVERSITY PRESS | University Park and London

1L + pp (3)–175, illus, 22cm.

1L, blank; p (3), Title-page; verso, Publication details; p (5), Dedication; verso blank; pp 7–8, List of Contents; pp 9–29, Introduction; p 30, blank; p 31, A note on the Texts and A note on the Endpaper Maps; p (32), blank; pp 33–171, Text; p (172), blank; pp 173–5, Index; + Endpaper maps taken from *Seven Pillars of Wisdom*.

The writings in this work all appeared in a series of newspaper and journal articles between 1918–21, some of them anonymous. The text follows the format of the original publication, including captions, and, where the pieces were signed, Lawrence's byline and the accompanying identification of the writer. The title article 'Evolution of a Revolt' appeared in a series of articles whilst *The Seven Pillars of Wisdom* was in the process of being revised and the final version of these articles formed part of the subscriber's edition of *The Seven Pillars of Wisdom*.

The introduction by the editors deals briefly with Lawrence's career prior to the peace conference, and more extensively with his writings after the peace conference, especially those relating to his campaign supporting the Arab cause. It also deals with the writing of *The Seven Pillars of Wisdom* and its reliance on the *Arab Bulletin* reports, and his handwritten notes and reports.

The Forest Giant, 1924, English Edition

THE FOREST GIANT | by | ADRIEN LE CORBEAU |
(device) | (rule) | Translated from the French by | J. H.
ROSS | (device) | JONATHAN CAPE | ELEVEN GOWER
STREET, LONDON

pp (1)–(160), 19½cm.

pp (1), and (2), blank; p (3), Half-title; p (4), Frontispiece; p (5),
Title-page; p 6, FIRST PUBLISHED IN MCMXXLIV |
MADE AND PRINTED IN GREAT BRITAIN | BY
BUTLER AND TANNER LTD | FROME AND |
LONDON | (Floret); p 7, Contents; p (8), blank; pp 9–158,
Text; pp (159–60), blank.

The Forest Giant, 1924, American Edition

(double rule) THE | FOREST GIANT | The Romance | of a
Tree | (rule) | *Translated from the French of* | ADRIEN LE
CORBEAU | by L. H. ROSS | (rule) (device) (quotation)
(double rule) Harper and Brothers | New York and London |
MCMXXIV

5Ls + pp 1–(140) + 1L.

L 1, blank; L 2, Half-title; verso, blank; Frontispiece; L 3, Title-
page; verso, (rule) THE FOREST GIANT | (rule) Copyright,
1924, by Harper and Brothers | Printed in the USA | (rule)
First Edition | A–Y; L 4, Contents; verso, blank; L 5, Half-
title; verso, blank; pp 1–139, Text; p (140), blank; L 6, blank.

J. H. Ross definitely appears as L. H. Ross on the title-page of

32

the Library of Congress copy. The copyright deposit was made
on 15 March 1924.

The Home Letters of T. E. Lawrence and his Brothers, 1954

THE HOME | LETTERS OF | T. E. LAWRENCE | AND
HIS   BROTHERS | BASIL   BLACKWELL | OXFORD |
1954

1L + pp (i)–xvi + pp (1)–(732) + 1L, 23½cm.

L 1, blank; p (i), Half-title; verso, blank; p (iii), Title-page;
p (iv), Printed in England etc; p v, Contents; p (vi), Acknow-
ledgements; p vii–viii, List of illustrations; p ix, Publisher's
note; p x, Note by M. R. Lawrence; p xi, Notes on the life of
T. E. Lawrence; p xii, Facsimile of letter from Winston
Churchill dated 4 March 1954; pp xiii–xvi, Address by Winston
Churchill at unveiling of the Memorial to Lawrence at Oxford
High School; p (1), Section title, T. E. Lawrence; verso, blank;
portrait; pp 3–392, Home letters of T. E. Lawrence; pp 393–722,
Home letters of W. G. and F. H. Lawrence; pp 723–7, Index to
T. E. Lawrence section; pp 728–31, Indexes to letters of W. G.
and F. H. Lawrence; L 2, blank.

Some of these letters previously appeared in David Garnett's
The Letters of T. E. Lawrence and *Selected Letters of T. E. Lawrence*,
though not all were printed in their entirety. Lawrence's letters
are, with some exceptions, literary exercises which reflected his
interest in the subjects about which he was writing, and they
provide an interesting background to Lawrence's other writings.
The section covering his letters from Carchemish are the most
impressive with their obvious enthusiasm for archaeology, the

C

countryside and its people, whereas those of the period during the war reveal, naturally enough, little of his actions.

The later letters are in part indicative of Lawrence's post-war disillusionment, mainly in the form of undertones, though when he was working on the translation of the Odyssey his state of mind was demonstrated by his intention never to undertake any more original work as 'It is not good for men to make things'. He was also pre-occupied with the problem of loneliness which he considered it impossible to be as it was '. . . the only experience that humanity has never really worked towards: and I'm quite sure we can only manage it in a crowded place. The difficulty is to keep oneself untouched in a crowd'. Also of interest are the letters relating to his work on the high-speed launches for rescue work, which had become his main interest.

The Letters of T. E. Lawrence, 1938

THE LETTERS | of | T. E. LAWRENCE | Edited by | DAVID GARNETT | (device) | LONDON | JONATHAN CAPE 30 BEDFORD SQUARE | AND AT TORONTO

1L + pp (1)–896 + 1L

L 1, blank; p (1), Half-title; verso, blank; p (3), blank; p (4), Frontispiece; p (5), Title-page; p (6), FIRST PUBLISHED 1938 | JONATHAN CAPE LTD, 30 BEDFORD SQUARE, LONDON | AND 91 WELLINGTON STREET WEST, TORONTO | PRINTED IN GREAT BRITAIN IN THE CITY OF OXFORD | AT THE ALDEN PRESS | PAPER MADE BY JOHN DICKINSON & CO LTD | BOUND BY A. W. BAIN & CO LTD; pp 7–24, Contents; pp 25–7, List of recipients of letters; p 28, blank; p 29, List of illustrations and maps; p 30, blank; pp 31–2, Preface; pp 33–4, Note on the text; p 35, PART ONE | ARCHAEOLOGY; p 36, blank; pp 37–41, Introduction to Part one; p 42, blank; pp 43–177, Letters; p 178, blank; p 179, PART TWO | THE WAR; p 180, blank; pp 181–4, Introduction to Part Two; pp 185–258, Letters; p 259, PART THREE | THE DOG FIGHT IN DOWNING STREET; p 260, blank; pp 261–4, Introduction to Part Three; pp 265–346, Letters; p 347, PART FOUR | THE YEARS OF HIDE AND SEEK | 1922–9; p 348, blank; pp 349–53, Introduction to Part Four; p 354, blank; pp 355–628, Letters; p 629, PART FIVE | FLYING BOATS; p 630, blank; pp 631–8, Introduction to Part Five; pp 639–873, Letters; p 874, blank; pp 875–96, Index; + 1 L, blank.

The letters are arranged within each section by date and each one is numbered consecutively. The list of recipients, pp 25–7, includes the numbers of the letters against each person's name but the addressee, as such, does not appear in the index. Where possible the transcripts of the letters were checked against the originals by Lawrence's trustees or by the editor, and this is indicated in the list of contents by T or G following the date of the letter. The editor has, by the use of footnotes, explained references not explained in the letters and related references in other letters.

The collection of letters is obviously a necessary part of any study of Lawrence's work, revealing, as they do, so much of the background to his life, his thinking and his work. It is a work to be used more for specific interests, and in this connection the letters to Edward Garnett regarding *The Seven Pillars of Wisdom* are of great interest. It is unfortunate that the work does not give a summary of the letters to which Lawrence is replying, and to gain the utmost value the work should be used with *Letters to T. E. Lawrence* (see p 103).

Letters to Bruce Rogers, 1933

LETTERS | FROM T. E. SHAW TO BRUCE ROGERS

33Ls (no signature, no pagination), 21¼cm.

Ls 1 and 2, blank; L 3, Title; verso, Copyright 1933 by Bruce Rogers | All rights reserved | 200 copies Privately Printed at the | press of William Edwin Rudge | from type set by Bertha M. Goudy; L 4, Foreword by Bruce Rogers; Ls 5-44, Text of letters.

These letters were written by Lawrence in connection with the translation of the Odyssey of Homer which was to be produced by Rogers.

Men in Print, 1940

MEN IN PRINT | ESSAYS IN LITERARY CRITICISM BY | T. E. LAWRENCE | INTRODUCTION BY | A. W. LAWRENCE | THE GOLDEN COCKEREL PRESS

2Ls + pp (2)–(60), 25½cm.

2Ls, blank; p 2, Title-page; verso, Printed in Great Britain; p (4), List of Contents; verso, blank; pp (6)–15, Introduction by A. W. Lawrence; p 16, blank; pp 17–59, Text; p (60), Printed in the midst of war by Christopher Sandford and Owen | Rutter at the Golden Cockerel Press, in Perpetua type on Arnold's | mould-made paper, and finished on the 16th day of July, 1940. The | Edition is limited to 500 numbered copies, of which Numbers 1–30 | are bound in full Niger and accompanied by a facsimile reproduction | of T. E. Lawrence's manuscript of one of the essays. Numbers 31–500 are bound in ¼ Niger. Number: 163.

The first thirty copies with the facsimile of Lawrence's manuscript of one of the essays also has the following:
(p 61), A Facsimile Reproduction | of T. E. Lawrence's Handwriting | The Manuscript of the Note on | James Elroy Flecker | Printed by the Collotype process, | this Supplement has been limited | to thirty copies to accompany the | first thirty copies of Men in Print; pp (63–7), Manuscript.

The collection consists of the following:
I A note on James Elroy Flecker.
  A brief portrait of Flecker whom Lawrence met at Beirut and their slowly growing friendship which was based on mutual respect. They corresponded with each other until Flecker's death and this essay was probably written in 1926.
II A review of novels by D. H. Lawrence.
  A review which appeared in *The Spectator* on 6 August 1927 over the initials C.D. which was the pseudonym 'chosen because Colindale was the last Tube Station I entered before going to India'.
III A review of the short stories of H. G. Wells.
  A review which appeared in *The Spectator* on 25 February 1928.
IV A criticism of Henry Williamson's *Tarka the Otter*, with some remarks on the style of Doughty's *Arabia Deserta*. The substance of a letter to Edward Garnett responding to a proof copy of *Tarka the Otter* in which Lawrence suggests changes, and comments generally on the book which he considered 'The best thing I've met for ever so long'. The note on Doughty is brief and really an aside to the comment on Williamson, though it makes some interesting points on

37

Doughty's style which Lawrence felt 'mirrored Doughty as much as it mirrored Arabia'.

V A review of the works of Walter Savage Landor.
A favourable review of the works of Landor published by Chapman & Hall in three volumes and which Lawrence felt would never be bettered either from the quality of the book or the suppressed presence of the editing.

The Mint, 1955, English Trade Edition

T. E. LAWRENCE | THE MINT | *A day-book of the RAF Depot between | August and December 1922 | with later notes | by | 352087 A/c ROSS | LONDON* | JONATHAN CAPE 30 BEDFORD SQUARE

1L + pp (1)–(2) + 3–206

L 1, Half-title; verso, ALSO BY T. E. LAWRENCE | *Crusader Castles | The Wilderness of Zin | Seven Pillars of Wisdom* | p (1), Title; p (2), FIRST PUBLISHED 1955 | PRINTED IN GREAT BRITAIN IN THE CITY OF OXFORD | AT THE ALDEN PRESS | PAPER BY JOHN DICKINSON & CO LTD | BOUND BY A. W. BAIN & CO LTD, LONDON | pp 3–5, Contents; p 6, blank; pp 7–10, Notes by A. W. Lawrence; p 11, PART ONE | THE RAW MATERIAL; p (12), To EDWARD GARNETT (etc); pp 13–206, Text.

At Lawrence's request, publication of this work was withheld until after 1950, except for an American edition of 1936 which was printed from the original manuscript and designed to secure copyright in America. Only fifty copies of this 1936 edition were printed and ten offered for sale for not less than $500,000 each. Two copies were deposited in the Library of Congress, one at the British Museum and a single copy sold to Lawrence's agent Raymond Savage for $1. In fact lawyers decided that this device probably was not enough to secure copyright because of the restricted publication. The 1955 trade edition was revised by Lawrence from the original manuscript, but further editing was done to exclude the 'coarse words automatic in barrack room speech'.

The book gives a picture of barrack-room life in the RAF and in particular Lawrence's reactions to his change in environment and status. The book received a very mixed response from the critics and many considered that the book was in fact a literary failure. At the same time the picture it presented seems to have been accurate because the manuscript impressed Trenchard, and worried him as well, in case it should fall into the wrong hands, namely someone who wished to attack the Air Force. Trenchard finished reading *The Mint* in the July of 1928 and wrote: 'I read every word of it. And I seemed to know what was coming each line, and I felt no soreness, no sadness, about your writing, and yet again I feel all of a tremble in case it gets out and into the hands of people who do not know life as it is.' (Trenchard Papers.)

Minorities, 1971

T. E. LAWRENCE | MINORITIES | (device) | EDITED BY | J. M. WILSON | WITH A PREFACE BY | C. DAY LEWIS | (device) | JONATHAN CAPE | THIRTY BEDFORD SQUARE, LONDON

pp (1)–272, 22cm.

p (1), Half-title; verso, books by T. E. Lawrence; frontispiece; p (3), Title-page; verso, first published etc; p (5), Contents;

verso, blank; pp 7–9, Acknowledgements; verso, blank; pp 11–12, Abbreviations used in the References; pp 13–16, Preface; pp 17–50, Introduction; p (51), blank; p 52, Note on Contents; pp 53–64, List of Poems; pp (65)–240, Minorities; pp (241)–265, Notes; p (266), blank; pp 267–8, Index of Authors; pp 269–272, Index of First Lines.

This collection of poems was Lawrence's private anthology which he copied into a small notebook to carry around with him. The poems were chosen by Lawrence for their content and in some cases for only a portion of the poem, and Wilson feels that though these poems are not necessarily good literary judgement, they do contain many of the ideas also expressed by Lawrence. The collection was given to Charlotte Shaw in 1927 in return for her own private anthology of meditations.

This work is most important because of the introduction by J. M. Wilson which represents a very detailed analysis of Lawrence based on years of study. Wilson considers that this collection of poems is an important source of biographical material on Lawrence because of the light that it throws on his mental state, especially during the crucial period between October 1918, after the fall of Damascus, and 1922 when *The Mint* was written. This study of Lawrence is a most important contribution to any study of Lawrence covering the identity of 'S.A.' (which Wilson feels was almost certainly Ahmed Dahoum, headman at Carchemish), his mental state following the peace settlement and his writings. In considering Lawrence's decision to enlist in the ranks, Wilson feels that there is no reason to doubt Lawrence's word that he had planned to do so in 1919 'but not till Winston had given the Arabs a fair deal was I free to please myself'. This he considered was achieved by the 1921 peace conference and so Lawrence enlisted in 1922. The reason, Wilson feels, was based on Lawrence's wartime experiences. Lawrence, in his letters to Robert Graves, wrote: 'these friendly outings with the armoured car and Air Force fellows were what persuaded me that my best future, if I survived the war, was to enlist'.

Many of Wilson's conclusions are at variance with some of Lawrence's biographers though 'These disagreements are not emphasized, since lengthy justification would distort the proportions of the narrative'.

More Letters to Bruce Rogers, 1936

MORE LETTERS | FROM T. E. SHAW TO BRUCE ROGERS

16Ls (no signatures, no pagination), 21¼cm.

L 1, blank; L 2, Title-page; verso, Copyright 1936 by Bruce Rogers | All Rights reserved | 300 copies Privately Printed | by permission of the | trustees of the late T. E. Shaw | Printed in USA; L 3, Introduction by Bruce Rogers; Ls 4–16, Text of letters.

The Odyssey of Homer, 1935

THE ODYSSEY OF | HOMER | TRANSLATED BY T. E. SHAW | (COLONEL T. E. LAWRENCE | (device) | OXFORD UNIVERSITY PRESS | LONDON: HUMPHREY MILFORD

(x), pp 1–327, 23½cm.

p (i), Half-title; verso, blank; p (iii), Title-page; verso, This Edition was published in the USA in 1932. It was first published in this form in England, 1935; pp (v)–(vii), Translator's Note; p (viii), blank; p (ix), Contents; verso, blank; pp (1)–327, Text.

In his note, Lawrence states that this is a translation made from the Oxford text, uncritically. The remainder of the note deals in a general way with the work of Homer and Lawrence's impressions. The translation was undertaken at the request of Bruce Rogers but he was not too happy about his capabilities for in one of his letters to Rogers he wrote: 'Something about this Odyssey effort frightens me. It's too big: Homer is very, very great: and so far away. It seems only a sort of game, to try to bring him down to the ordinary speech of my mouth. Yet that is what a translation ought to mean.'

PUBLICATION NOTE

Limited Edition: 1932	Bruce Rogers Printing 530 copies
Book of the Month Club: 1932	Six copies only printed in New York.
Review Copies: 1932	25 review copies printed in New York by OUP.
American Limited Edition: 1932	34 copies printed in New York.
American Trade Edition: 1932	
American Popular Edition: 1934	
English Trade Edition: 1935	As described above.

Oriental Assembly, 1939, English Edition

ORIENTAL | ASSEMBLY | by | T. E. Lawrence | (device) | Edited by | A. W. LAWRENCE | *With Photographs by* | *The Author* | London | WILLIAMS AND NORGATE LTD | GREAT RUSSELL STREET

1L + (i)–(xiv) + 1–(292), 22cm.

L 1, Half-title; verso, blank; p (i), blank; p (ii), frontispiece; p (iii), Title-page; p (iv), FIRST PUBLISHED IN GREAT BRITAIN IN 1939 | PRINTED IN GREAT BRITAIN BY NEILL AND CO LTD, EDINBURGH; p v, FOREWORD by A. W. Lawrence; p (vi), blank; p vii, Contents; p (viii), blank; pp ix–xii, List of Illustrations; p (xiii), 1 | DIARY OF A JOURNEY | ACROSS THE EUPHRATES; p (xiv), blank; pp 1–4, Editor's note; pp 5–(64), Text; 18 leaves of unpaginated plates; pp 65–157, Text; p (158), blank; p 159, VI | THE WAR | PHOTOGRAPHS; p 160, blank; pp 161–2, Editor's note; pp 163–4, Index; p (165), blank; pp 166–291, plates.

This volume contains Lawrence's miscellaneous writings with the exception of *Crusader Castles* (Editor's foreword). The contents of the work are as follows:

1 'Diary of a journey across the Euphrates' (see p 28).
2 'The Changing East' (reprinted from *Roundhouse* where it appeared anonymously in 1920). An essay on the changes taking place in the political and social structure of the Middle East.
3 *The Evolution of a Revolt* (see p 59, *Army Quarterly* and p 31, *Evolution of a Revolt*, edited by Weintraub).
4 The suppressed introductory chapter for *Seven Pillars of Wisdom* (see comments by Weintraub in *Private Shaw and Public Shaw*, p 121).
5 On Eric Kennington's Arab portraits (for Kennington's account, see p 145).
6 The war photographs. These form part of Lawrence's collection of war photographs with the exception of those presented to the Imperial War Museum. The photographs are arranged in the order in which the subjects are mentioned

in *The Seven Pillars of Wisdom* and the spelling of the Arabic names conforms to that used in the book's index.

Revolt in the Desert, 1927

REVOLT IN THE DESERT | by | T. E. LAWRENCE | (device) | LONDON | JONATHAN CAPE, 30 BEDFORD SQUARE | 1927

1L + pp (1)–(446) + map, illus, 23½cm.

L 1, Half-title; verso, blank; frontispiece; p (1), Title-page; verso, PRINTED IN GREAT BRITAIN; pp (3)–(4), Contents; pp (5)–(6), List of illustrations; pp (7)–(8), Publisher's note; p (9), Foreword by T. E. Lawrence; verso, blank; pp (11)–(435), Text; verso, blank; pp (437)–(446), Index; + map.

Revolt in the Desert is an abridgement of *The Seven Pillars of Wisdom*. It was the only version available to the general public until the 1935 edition of *The Seven Pillars of Wisdom* was issued for general circulation. The book was published mainly to enable Lawrence to clear the debts left by the production of the subscriber's edition of *The Seven Pillars of Wisdom* and the rest of the profit was given to the RAF Memorial Fund.

The book was offered to Cape with the proviso that Lawrence could withdraw the book when he considered that it had made enough money. Work on the abridgement lasted three months and was the result of drastic editing: 'He took a set of the subscriber's sheets and, with a brush and indian ink, boldly obliterated whole slabs of text. The first seven chapters—he dropped in their entirety. Later cuts removed many consecutive pages, and an occasional whole chapter. From 652 pages of printed text, 211 were cut out altogether' (Michael S. Howard,

Works by Lawrence

Jonathan Cape, Publisher). In the main these cuts were material
of a personal or reflective nature and what was left required
only a minor amount of linking material.

This is an extremely readable account of the Arab Revolt and
of Lawrence's part in it although one should remember the
various inaccuracies which have since come to light. It is an
easier work to read than the *Seven Pillars*, mainly because the
reflective material and the personal insights have been omitted.
The book was an instant success as is testified to by Michael S.
Howard (see p 96).

PUBLICATION NOTE:
English Limited Edition: 315 copies printed of which 300
1927   were for sale.
English Trade Edition: 1927   As described above.
American Limited Edition:
1927   250 copies printed.
American Trade Edition: Published by George H. Doran
1927   Co.
See Appendix for details of the writing and publication of *The
Seven Pillars of Wisdom*.

Secret Despatches from Arabia, 1939

SECRET DESPATCHES | FROM ARABIA | BY T. E.
LAWRENCE | Published by Permission | of the Foreign
Office | Foreword by | A. W. Lawrence | THE GOLDEN
COCKEREL PRESS

1L + pp (1)–173 + 2 Ls, 25½cm.

1 L, blank; p (1), blank; verso, Portrait of Lawrence; p 3, Title-
page; verso, Printed in England; pp 5–7, Foreword; p (8),

blank; pp 9–10, List of contents; pp 11–171, Text; pp 172–3, Glossary; verso, blank; 1 L, Printed by Christopher Sandford and Owen Rutter at the Golden | Cockerel Press in Perpetua type on Arnold's mould-made paper. The | Edition is limited to 1,000 numbered copies, of which numbers 1–30 | are bound in white pig-skin and accompanied by a collotype reproduc- | tion of part of T. E. Lawrence's manuscript of 'The Seven Pillars of | Wisdom'. Numbers 31–1,000 are bound in ¼ Niger. Number: 571.

In his foreword to this collection, A. W. Lawrence states that this material was included in the *Arab Bulletin*, which was issued in Cairo from 6 June 1916 to 6 December 1918. The attribution of anonymous articles which appeared in the earlier issues of the *Bulletin* to T. E. Lawrence is based on the annotations that appear in his own copy.

The article on p 155, 'Syrian cross-currents', was written by Lawrence on Arab Bureau paper in 1918 but was not published in the *Bulletin*. The item is reproduced from the MSS in A. W. Lawrence's possession. *The Arab Bulletin* was the secret intelligence summary of the Arab Bureau and represents various reports collected by the members of the bureau (cf Gertrude Bell, *The Arab War*, p 171). The topics discussed are extremely varied and range from the religious views of Hussein to military operations against the Hedjaz railway, and because of their secret nature, have an honesty of approach. The collection includes Lawrence's thoughts on the treatment of the Arabs by British officers, entitled 'Twenty Seven Articles', designed to act as a guide 'for beginners in the Arab armies'.

The article, 'Syrian cross-currents', deals with the position of Syria in relation to the Arab Revolt and the Turkish control of Syria. It concluded that the Syrians would only be interested in obtaining their freedom if it were achieved by someone else and

'They would so much rather the Judean hills were stained with London Territorials, dead for their freedom, to save them from the need of taking dangerous rides'. Lawrence also felt that 'a spontaneous rebellion in Syria is an impossibility: the local people will take no action till the front tide of battle has rolled past them'. These charges are refuted by Suleiman Mousa in an article entitled 'The Role of Syrians and Iraqis in the Arab Revolt (see p 151).

Seven Pillars of Wisdom, Miscellaneous

To Subscribers to *The Seven Pillars of Wisdom*, 1925

My estimate of the time required to produce an adequate edition of my war narrative *The Seven Pillars*, has proved wrong . . .

A single sheet date 1 June 1925; sent to subscribers to explain the delay in publication and enclosing a specimen page of the first draft of 1922.

Some notes on the writing of The Seven Pillars of Wisdom *by* T. E. Shaw

Four pages issued to those who bought, or were presented with copies of the 1926 edition.

Sample pages of The Seven Pillars of Wisdom

(Np, nd) pp 1–40, with coloured plate of Ghalib as frontis.

The Seven Pillars of Wisdom, 1926, Private Edition

THE SEVEN PILLARS | OF | WISDOM | a triumph | 1926

Map + pp (i)–xxii + pp (1)–660 + maps and plates, 25½cm.

Map; pp (i), and (ii), blank; p (iii), Title; p (iv), blank; Frontis-piece; p (v), Dedicatory Poem to S.A.; p (vi), 'T.E.S. | Cran-well. 15.8.26; pp vii–xviii, Synopsis; pp xix–xxii, List of Illustrations; p (1), blank; pp (2)–659, Text; p (660), Text and decorations printed by Manning Pike with the assistance | of H. J. Hodgson at 25 Charles Street, London, W.11. | Plates by Charles Whittingham and Griggs.

Lawrence decided that this subscribers' edition of *The Seven Pillars* should be an edition-de-luxe and consequently he gave full rein to his typographic and illustrative ideas, regardless of cost. Only about 100 copies were produced at 30 guineas each. An 'incomplete' edition of this work was produced for men who served with Lawrence in Arabia, and these were given by the author. This edition lacked several of the plates that appeared in the subscribers' edition.

In some copies a few of the illustrations are missing, while others contain a plate, 'The Prickly Pear', following the text, not included in the list at the beginning. In certain copies two line drawings by Paul Nash, 'Prophet's Tomb' and 'A Garden', listed as appearing on pp 92 and 208, are in fact omitted.

The Seven Pillars of Wisdom, 1926, American Edition

THE SEVEN | PILLARS OF WISDOM | NEW YORK: | George H. Doran Company | MCMXXVI

2Ls + pp (1)–652 + 2Ls.

D

L 1, Title; verso, COPYRIGHT, 1926 | By George H. Doran Company; L 2, blank; p (1), blank; pp 2-652, Text; L 3, Of this book there | have been printed | and bound twenty- | two copies, each one of | which is numbered and | signed by the publisher and | only ten of | which are for sale. | *This copy number* -; verso, blank; L 4, blank.

The Library of Congress copy is not numbered. The copyright deposit was made on 3 December 1926.

The Seven Pillars of Wisdom, 1935, American Limited Edition

SEVEN PILLARS | OF WISDOM | a triumph | T. E. LAWRENCE | GARDEN CITY, NEW YORK | DOUBLEDAY, DORAN AND COMPANY, INC | MCMXXXV

1 L + pp (1)-672.

L 1, THIS EDITION IS LIMITED TO | SEVEN HUNDRED AND FIFTY COPIES | OF WHICH THIS IS | No -; verso, blank; p (1), Half-title; p (2), blank; Frontispiece; p (3), Title; p (4), Printed at the *Country Life Press*, Garden City, NY, USA | Privately Printed 1926 | First Published for general circulation, 1935 | Copyright 1926, 1935 | By DOUBLEDAY, DORAN AND COMPANY, INC | All Rights Reserved | FIRST EDITION; p (5), To S.A.; p (6), T.E.S. | Cranwell, 15.8.26; pp 7-18, Synopsis; pp 19, 20, Illustrations; Facsimile of a page of the MS of Text III; pp 21, 22, Preface by A. W. Lawrence; Facsimile on a page of the text printed at Oxford 1922; pp 23, 24, Preface (cont); Facsimile of A page of the Subscribers' text, abridged | by the author for *Revolt in the Desert*; pp 25, 26, Preface (cont); p (27), Half-title: pp (28)- (661), Text; pp 662-6, Appendices; pp 667-72, Index.

The Library of Congress copy is not numbered. The copyright deposit was made on 1 October 1935.

The Seven Pillars of Wisdom, 1935, English Trade Edition

SEVEN PILLARS | OF WISDOM | a triumph | T. E. LAWRENCE | LONDON | JONATHAN CAPE 30 BEDFORD SQUARE | and at Toronto

pp (1)–672, 26cm.

p (1), Half-title; verso, blank; Frontispiece; p (3), Title-page; verso, PRIVATELY PRINTED 1926 | FIRST PUBLISHED FOR GENERAL CIRCULATION | 1935 | PRINTED IN GREAT BRITAIN IN THE CITY OF OXFORD | AT THE ALDEN PRESS | ILLUSTRATIONS IN PHOTO-GRAVURE | BY JOHN SWAIN & SON, LTD | MAPS BY THE CHISWICK PRESS, LTD | PAPER BY JOHN DICKINSON & CO, LTD | BOUND BY A. W. BAIN & CO, LTD; p (5) Dedication to S.A.; p (6), T. E. S. Cranwell, 15.8.26; pp 7–18, Synopsis; pp 19–20, Illustrations; pp 21–6, Preface by A. W. Lawrence; p (27), Half-title; pp (28)–661, Text; pp 662–6, Appendices; pp 667–72, Index.

Shaw-Ede: T. E. Lawrence's Letters to H. S. Ede, 1927–1935, 1942

SHAW-EDE | T. E. LAWRENCE'S LETTERS | TO H. S. EDE | 1927–1935 | FOREWORD AND RUNNING COMMENTARY BY | H. S. EDE | THE GOLDEN COCKEREL PRESS

2Ls + pp (3)–62 + 2Ls, 25½cm.

2Ls, blank; p (3), Title-page; verso, PRINTED IN GREAT BRITAIN; p 5, Foreword; verso, blank; pp 7–61, Text; p 62, Printed by Christopher Sandford and Owen Rutter at the Golden | Cockerel Press, Rolls Passage, London EC4; in 14 pt Perpetua type on | Arnold's mould-made paper, and finished on the 4th day of September, | 1942. The edition is limited to 500 numbered copies, of which num- | bers 1–30 are bound in full morocco and accompanied by facsimile re- | productions of five of the letters. Numbers 31–500 are bound in | ¼ morocco. Number: 266

This correspondence was motivated by a visit Ede made to an exhibition of the pictures used to illustrate *The Seven Pillars of Wisdom*, held at the Leicester Galleries in May 1927. This exhibition prompted Ede to read *Revolt in the Desert* and subsequently to write to Lawrence.

A great deal of the correspondence is concerned with criticism of Ede's work and Lawrence's responses to Ede's observations on his own work. The letters also provide an insight into Lawrence's life in the RAF and his life in general. A letter to Ede written at Clouds Hill on 5 April 1935 declined his offer of money, due to Lawrence's desire to discover whether he had earned enough to live in decency: 'My earning power is potentially considerable: but I hate using it'. The whole tone of the letter is concerned with Lawrence's retirement which he wanted to enjoy as he felt 'that I have worked throughout a reasonably long working life, given all I can to every cause which harnessed me, and earned a rest'. Shortly after this letter Lawrence died without enjoying the rest which he sought.

T. E. Lawrence to his Biographers Robert Graves and Liddell Hart, 1963

T. E. LAWRENCE | TO HIS BIOGRAPHERS | Robert Graves | AND | Liddell Hart | (Device) | CASSELL LONDON

pp (i)–(x) + pp 1–260

p (i), Half-title; verso, blank; frontispiece; p (iii), Title-page; p (iv), CASSELL & COMPANY LTD | 35 Red Lion Square London WC1 | etc | T. E. LAWRENCE TO HIS BIO-GRAPHER, ROBERT GRAVES | Copyright 1938 by Inter-national Authors N.V. | T. E. LAWRENCE TO HIS BIO-GRAPHER LIDDELL HART | Copyright 1938 by Double-day & Company Inc | © This edition 1963 | etc; p (v), T. E. Lawrence | TO HIS BIOGRAPHER | ROBERT GRAVES | *Information about himself, in the form of letters, notes and answers to questions, edited with a critical commentary*; p vi, PUBLISHER'S NOTE | *Unless they are specifically attributed to T. E. Lawrence, all footnotes | throughout this section are by Robert Graves. The letters L.H. before | page references indicate the com-panion work by Liddell Hart*; pp vii–(viii), Foreword by Robert Graves; p ix, Contents; verso, blank; pp (1)–187, Text; p 188, blank.

p (i), T. E. Lawrence | TO HIS BIOGRAPHER | LIDDELL HART | *Information about himself, in the form of letters, notes, answers to | questions and conversations*; p ii, PUBLISHER'S NOTE | *ON pages 77–124, 147–62 and 174–85 references to matter in the | typescript on Captain Liddell Hart's book, T. E. Lawrence: in | Arabia and After, together with references in the corresponding | pages of the published book on which this matter may be found, are | given in this way: 'T.3, B.16(5)', which means that the matter | commented upon was on p 3 of the typescript and may be found on p 16 | of the Cape edition of the book and on p 5 of the Dodd, Mead edition. | (The book was published in England by Jonathan Cape, | Ltd, in the United States by Dodd, Mead & Co, under the title,* Colonel Lawrence, The Man Behind the Legend*). T. E. Law- | rence's comments | and changes, set in smaller type, | follow the matter quoted from the typescript. In general, all Lawrence's letters and his answers to Captain Liddell Hart's questions, etc, are set in | the smaller type. Throughout this section the footnotes are by Captain | Liddell Hart, except where they are specifically attributed to T. E. | Lawrence. The letters R.G. before page references indicate the | companion work by Robert Graves;* pp iii–iv, Foreword by Liddell Hart; pp (1)–233, Text; p (234), blank; pp 235–60, Index.

The publisher's notes have been shown in full because they are important to a full understanding of the text and its layout. One index covers both parts of the work with references in bold roman numerals to differentiate between the sections.

Contributions to Newspapers and Periodicals

All contributions are arranged alphabetically by title, except the series of articles that appeared in the *Daily Telegraph* and *The Worlds Work*, which are arranged in order of appearance as they show the development of the Arab Revolt.

'Among the Bedouins'
Empire News (Manchester), 9 June 1935, p 7.

'The Arab campaign, land and sea operations, British Navy's help'
The Times (London), 26 November 1918, p 5 (not signed)

This article deals with Feisal's unsuccessful attempt to take Medina and the resultant advance of the Turks on Mecca which was foiled by the attack on Wejh. This attack was greatly assisted by the transportation provided by the Navy which carried Feisal's army from Yenbo to Um Lejj some half way up the Hedjaz coast towards Wejh. Whilst the main body of troops made their way from Um Lejj to Wejh by land, a small party was landed by the Navy and this party had, with the assistance of the Navy guns, nearly completed the assault by the time Feisal's main army arrived. The Navy then transported other parties further up the coast, thus enabling nearly all of the northern part of the Red Sea to Akaba to be cleared of Turkish forces.

In this article Lawrence lays particular stress on the part played by the Navy and on the co-operation of Admiral Wemyss and other senior officers who took an active and constructive interest in the operations.

'The Arab Epic, Doom of Turk power in Syria, wrecking the Hedjaz railway'
The Times (London), 28 November 1918, p 4 (not signed)

The article concludes the story of the Arab Revolt though it omits the Arab attack on Maan and the final advance on Damascus. The article deals with the minor skirmishes and attacks on the railway which took place during the winter of 1917–18. In the main these were only isolated incidents as winter prevented any major advances being made by either side.

'The Arab epic: Feisal's battles in the desert, on the threshold of Syria'
The Times (London), 27 November 1918, p 7 (not signed)

This article takes up the story of the Arab Revolt from the capture of Wejh and deals with Feisal's forming of a regular army whilst at the same time continuing the attacks on the Hedjaz railway. It goes on to consider the impact that Sheik Auda abu Tayi of the Howeitat had on the army and the propaganda value he gave to the cause. In his description of the forming of the alliance is a remarkable picture of a real brigand of the desert made more human by the story of Auda's false teeth. 'Halfway through the meal he (Auda) rose with an apology, and withdrew from the tent. We heard a noise of hammering without, and saw Auda beating something between two great stones. When he came back he craved pardon of the Sheik for having inadvertently eaten bread with Turkish teeth, and displayed the broken remains of his rather fine Damascus set in his hand.'

Lawrence continues with a description of the taking of Akaba which was only captured after a severe struggle in which Nasir and Auda played prominent parts. After the taking of Akaba, Lawrence travelled, with a small bodyguard, to Suez to deliver news of the event and to arrange for food and money to be sent from Cairo by sea. It was during the advance from Wejh to Akaba that Lawrence went on the spying trip to Damascus which has been the subject of much controversy, and in fact Suleiman Mousa refutes Lawrence's story based on the testimony of Arabs who maintained that he never left the camp. Once again this is another part of the Lawrence legend which has not been satisfactorily solved.

'Arab rights: Our policy in Mesopotamia'
The Times (London), 23 July 1920, p 15

A letter to *The Times* signed T. E. Lawrence, All Souls College, 22 July, discussing the Arab Revolt in Mesopotamia. The letter was motivated by the debate on the situation in the House of Commons and articles in the press expressing surprise at the events. It seemed to Lawrence to be based on a misconception of the New Asia and the history of the previous five years '. . . I would like to trespass at length on your space and give my interpretation of the situation'.

The first cause of unrest was, according to Lawrence, the continuance of the military administration, a government in which the Arabs had no voice and the presence of a garrison of six figures costing £50 million. The solution to the problem, Lawrence felt, was to allow the Arabs a greater say in the government and to permit them to form volunteer units to keep law and order. 'I believe the Arabs in these conditions would be as loyal as anyone in the Empire, and they would not cost us a cent. . . . Of course, there is oil in Mesopotamia, but we are no nearer that while the Middle East remains at war, and I think if it is so necessary for us, it could be the subject of a bargain. The Arabs seem willing to shed their blood for freedom; how much more their oil!'

'Campaign of the Caliphs for Damascus: Story of the desert fighting from Mecca to Damascus under the King of the Hedjaz' *Current History* (a monthly magazine of the *New York Times*), February 1919, pp 348–57

(review) 'A critic of critics criticised' *The Spectator* (London), 27 August 1927, pp 321–2 (signed C.D., ie Colin Dale, one of Lawrence's pseudonyms)

(review) 'D. H. Lawrence's novels' *The Spectator* (London), 6 August 1927, p 223

'Demolitions under Fire' *The Royal Engineers' Journal*, XXIX, January 1919

Deals, in a technical form, with the methods used by Lawrence in demolition attacks on the Hedjaz railway. It deals with the best method of mining railways and bridges and the results achieved by using varied sizes of charges and their positioning.

'Emir Feisal, Creator of the Arab Army, A modern Saladin'
The Times (London), 7 August 1920, p 9

The article begins by setting the scene of the problems faced at
the Paris peace talks and especially the hostility of the French
towards Arab aspirations which were considered to be a device
to extend the sphere of British influence. It then describes
Feisal's upbringing and his activities prior to the Arab Revolt,
ending with his creation of an Arab regular army which he
moulded together despite their technical weakness against
organised armies. In addition he also moulded together the
various tribes who abandoned their traditional rivalries as a
result of his 'mediation, by reconciliation, by his personal
appeals, by setting before the people in impassioned address the
ideal of national union to win national freedom from the
Turks'.

'Emir Feisal, II. The Sykes-Picot Treaty, Impatient Arabs'
The Times (London), 11 August 1920, p 9

In this article Lawrence follows the successes of Feisal by dealing
with the falling away of Arab support for his leadership and his
ultimate downfall. After the fall of Akaba, Feisal's army was
comprised not of the Bedouin, who had returned to the Hedjaz,
but of Syrian tribesmen and villagers. This meant that when
Feisal refused to fight against the French occupation of Syria, he
was at odds with his own supporters. Feisal attempted to steer a
middle of the road policy regarding the French, the troubles in
Mesopotamia and the Palestinian Arabs' complaints concerning
the Jews. This policy cost him the support of many of his
followers who wished him to take arms against the French in
Syria, the British in Mesopotamia and the Jews in Palestine 'and
he must feel it rather ironic that his downfall came by the very
violence he had promised not to use'.

'The Evolution of a revolt'
Army Quarterly (London), Vol 1, No 1, October 1920, pp 55–69

This article by Lawrence is an examination of the military strategy of the Arab Revolt and is a clear explanation of the tactics adopted by the Arab armies in the struggle against the Turks. Lawrence begins by considering the early part of the Arab Revolt from which he drew the conclusion that it was not possible to oppose the Turks in the recognised military pattern. The essence of the Arab strategy had to be the stretching of Turkish resources over a wide area without entering into a conventionally fought battle.

Lawrence's strategy involved using the Arab army as a guerrilla force to harass the Turkish forces and to keep their forces stretched to breaking point as the only gain from a pitched battle to the Arabs 'was the ammunition the enemy fired off. Our victory lay not in battles, but in occupying square miles of country. . . . We had nothing material to lose, so we were to defend nothing and to shoot nothing.' In considering the criteria necessary for the success of the rebellion, Lawrence expresses his thesis for success in lucid terms which can be summarised as follows:

1 An unassailable base safe from attack and the fear of attack.
2 A sophisticated alien enemy with a disciplined army of occupation too small to dominate the country effectively.
3 A friendly population not necessarily totally active but with the non-active percentage being sympathetic.
4 The rebel force must be mobile and with endurance and good lines of supply.
5 The rebel force must have the equipment to paralyse the enemy's communication.

The article concludes that 'victory will rest with the insurgents, for the algebraical factors are in the end decisive, and against them perfections of means and spirit struggle quite in vain'.

'Four pledges to the Arabs'
The Times (London), 11 September 1919, p 11

This letter from Lawrence refers to the British promises to the French and the Arabs, and discusses Britain's promise to King Hussein, dated 24 October 1915; The Sykes-Picot agreement of May 1916; The British statement to seven Syrians at Cairo on 11 June 1917; and finally the Anglo-French Declaration of 9 November 1918. All of these documents are quoted to substantiate Lawrence's claim that Britain broke her pledges to the Arabs although his claim to be 'possibly the only informed *free-lance* [my italics] European' is somewhat suspect.

'France, Britain and the Arabs'
The Observer, 8 August 1920

Discusses Feisal's overthrow by the French and Britain's policy in Mesopotamia which Lawrence maintained was no better than that of France's towards Syria.

(review) 'Hakluyt—First naval propagandist'
The Spectator (London), 10 September 1927, pp 390–1 (signed C.D.)

'Massacre: Being a chapter from the history of the Arab Revolt'
The White Owl (London), No 3, 1923, pp 5–13

'Mesopotamia: The truth about the campaign'
The Sunday Times (London), 22 August 1920, p 7

'The Middle East. How we are losing prestige, Vacillating policy'
The Sunday Times (London), 30 May 1920, p 11

An article by Lawrence criticising the situation in the Middle East which he felt was a direct result of Britain's military administration which was retained ostensibly because of the delay in framing a peace treaty with Turkey. Lawrence then goes on to examine Britain's standing in the Middle East and concludes that because of her policy, Britain's standing was lower than it was at the end of the war.

The article examines the situation in Persia where Britain had concluded an agreement with the Shah contrary to the wishes of the people, and also infringing Persia's neutrality towards Russia 'by using Persia as a base for expeditions—one against Russian Turkestan, one against the Caspian . . . Lord Curzon assured his colleagues that these two brigades were holding Persia quiet, and stemming the Bolshevik flood in Asia. They must be remarkable brigades!' In Turkey, Lawrence felt that British support for the Sultan was doomed to failure as the real rulers of Turkey were the nationalist party led by Mustafa Kemal Pasha. In considering the situation in Syria and the role played by Feisal, Lawrence felt that only Feisal's self control and moderation 'had delayed our settling Syria by a military expedition. . . . It was not for such policies I fought.'

(review) 'Mixed Biscuits'
The Spectator (London), 20 August 1927, pp 290–1 (signed C.D.)

'Myself by Lawrence' (countersigned T. E. Shaw)
Evening Standard (London), 20 May 1935, pp 1–4

This manuscript, called by Shaw his epitaph, is printed with an article from Robert Graves called 'How this document was written'.

'Revolt in the Desert'
Daily Telegraph (London)
    I Seeking a prophet   15 December 1926

'Secrets of the war on Mecca'
Daily Express (London), 28 May 1920

An article in which Lawrence deals with the trouble between Hussein and Ibn Saud which had been deferred during the Middle East War. Initially the problem was one of religion, as the Wahabi movement of Ibn Saud's was a puritanical approach to Islam opposed to what he considered the corruptness of the Hedjaz society. As part of this desire to establish a purer form of religion, Ibn Saud was committed to taking and controlling Mecca, the centre of Islam, and it was this attempt to capture Mecca which led to the concern of the great powers.

Lawrence advised the Cabinet to support Hussein and accordingly, after much deliberation, Feisal was asked to undertake the defence of Mecca but he refused. Apparently, according to Lawrence, Feisal had offered to do this in 1918 and asked for armaments for the purpose. 'There had then ensued the usual three-part comedy and the Foreign Office pressing, the War Office hovering, the India Office opposing . . . and after six months' correspondence they offered their tanks too late for Feisal's convenience.' Lawrence felt that the policy of trying to reconcile Hussein and Ibn Saud could only be a temporary measure as it could not stop a new religion, and that if a solution were to be found it would 'involve that most difficult thing, agreement between three Government departments'.

'Service life: a few pages from unpublished notebooks of Lawrence of Arabia'
British Legion Journal (London), Vol 13, No 5, 1933, pp 160–1 & 169

'Two unpublished letters to Ezra Pound'
Nine (London), No 4, 1950, pp 180–2

'The War of the Departments'
Daily Express (London), 29 May 1920

In this article which was intended to be a sequel to 'Secrets of the War on Mecca', Lawrence again discusses the problems caused by the disagreement between the Foreign Office, The War Office and the India Office. In considering this problem he also puts forward what he felt was the underlying problem that those concerned with the Middle East of that time were 'those who have been viceroys or governors long ago'.

(review) 'The Wells Short Stories'
The Spectator (London), 25 February 1928, pp 368–9

'With Feisal at court and afield: 1. Adventures in Arabia with the Prince of the Hedjaz and the desert tribes'

The Worlds Work (New York), Vol XLII, No 3, July 1921, pp 277–88

'Arabian nights and days: A second chapter from a hitherto unpublished personal record of the Arab Revolt and conflicts with the Turk.'
The Worlds Work (New York), Vol XLII, No 4, August 1921, pp 381–6

'Arabian nights and days: III. A camel charge and other adventures in the desert'
The Worlds Work (New York), Vol XLII, No 5, September 1921, pp 516–20.

'Adventures in Arabia's deliverance: The Turkish army passes'
The Worlds Work (New York), Vol XLII, No 6, October 1921, pp 617–21.

These articles are interesting because they are part of an eight-chapter abridgement of one of the early versions of *Seven Pillars*, the manuscript from which evolved the article 'Evolution of a Revolt' (see p 59). In his introduction to Lawrence's post war writings collected under the title *Evolution of a Revolt* (see p 31), Stanley Weintraub compares the texts of these articles with the 1926 text of *Seven Pillars* to indicate 'the trend towards heightened "literary" and dramatic effects, some apparently products of a creative imagination rather than corrections in a chronicle'.

Section B

Miscellaneous writings by T. E. Lawrence, and works written in collaboration with others, including material in the Public Record Office

Custot, Pierre
'Sturly', by Pierre Custot, trs by Richard Aldington
London: Cape, 1924

Dust-jacket blurb by T. E. Lawrence. For attribution of dust-jacket to Lawrence see 'T. E. Lawrence by his Friends', article by Jonathan Cape, p 468.

Doughty, Charles M.
'Travels in Arabia Deserta', by Charles M. Doughty, with an introduction by T. E. Lawrence
London: Cape, 1921, 2 vols

Introduction by Lawrence, pp xxv–xxxv

This was a work which influenced much of Lawrence's early outlook about the Arabs. He studied it for a period of ten years, and came to feel that it was 'a bible of its kind', containing more information about the Arabs than any other work on the subject.

Publication Note

Cheaper Edition	2 vols	Jonathan Cape, 1923
1 vol edition		Jonathan Cape, 1926
1 vol edition		Boni & Liveright, New York, 1926
2 vol definitive edition		Jonathan Cape, 1936
2 vol definitive edition		Random House, New York, 1937

Garnett, Richard
'The Twilight of the Gods and other Tales', by Richard Garnett, with an introduction by T. E. Lawrence, illustrated by Henry Keen
London: John Lane The Bodley Head, 1924

xviii, 279 pp, illus, notes, 24½cm.

The introduction by Lawrence, pp vii–xiv, is as much a tribute to the British Museum as a critique on Garnett's book.

Jesty, Simon
'River Niger': a novel by Simon Jesty, with a prefatory letter by T. E. Lawrence
London: Boriswood, 1935

pp 11–13, Prefatory letter by T. E. Lawrence, 13 Birmingham Street, Southampton, T. E. S.

'Her Privates We', by Private 19022
Pamphlet issued by Peter Davies Ltd

This book had been well received by the critics and the public with much being made of the anonymity of the author. This pamphlet reproduces the text of a telephone conversation between Lawrence and Peter Davies and the substance of a letter from Lawrence concerning the book in which he wrote: '. . . anyone would be proud to have written it. It justifies every heat of praise. Its virtues will be recognised more and more as time goes on.'

Leicester Galleries, Catalogue of an Exhibition, 1927

CATALOGUE OF AN EXHIBITION | OF PAINTINGS, PASTELS, DRAWINGS | AND WOODCUTS | Illustrating Col T. E. LAWRENCE'S | book 'Seven Pillars of Wisdom' | With Prefaces by BERNARD SHAW | and T. E. LAWRENCE | ERNEST BROWN & PHILLIPS | THE LEICESTER GALLERIES | LEICESTER SQUARE, LONDON | EXHIBITION No 427 FEBRUARY 5th–21st, 1927

2Ls + pp (1)–(28) + 2 Ls, 14cm.

L 1, blank; L 2, Recto, Catalogue jacket; verso, Advertisement; pp (1)–(4), Advertisements; frontispiece; p (5), Title-page; verso, Advertisement; pp 7–13, Preface by George Bernard Shaw; pp 14–18, The following extract is from a note on Mr Kenning- | ton's Arab portraits written by Colonel Lawrence in | 1921; pp 19–27, Catalogue; p 28, Advertisement; L 3, Catalogue jacket with advertisements; L 4, blank.

This copy of the paper catalogue was bound by the London Library and Ls 1 & 4 are not part of the original catalogue.

Rich, Barbara
'No Decency Left', by Barbara Rich
London: Cape, 1932

pp 153–4 (Description of an autogiro)
For attribution see 'T. E. Lawrence by his Friends', p 579.

Thomas, Bertram
'Arabia Felix: Across the Empty Quarter of Arabia', by Bertram Thomas, with a foreword by T. E. Lawrence (T.E.S.)
London: Jonathan Cape, 1932

pp (i)–(xxxii), (1)–397, illus. maps, 23cm.

Foreword by Lawrence pp (xv)–(xviii)
Lawrence's reason for writing this foreword was his feeling that Thomas represented the end of an epoch—the traveller who made his exploration on foot and using his own resources. Also he relived through Thomas' book 'that wide land which I liked so much, twenty years ago, and hoped never to feel again'.

United Features Syndicate, Rare Books etc, 1937
Catalogue of an Exhibition and Sale at the American Art
Association Anderson Galleries Inc, 30 East 57th Street,
New York

This is a catalogue of an exhibition and sale held on Thursday
and Friday, 14 and 15 April 1937, and includes manuscripts,
maps, photographs and other memorabilia by and about
Colonel T. E. Lawrence. The material sold at this sale was from
the collection of Edward Robinson, who accompanied Lawrence during the Arab Revolt and produced a biography,
Lawrence the Rebel, in 1946 (see p 114). Material relating to
Lawrence appears between pp 109 and 124; the copy examined
is in the London Library.

Items listed in the catalogue
245 Lawrence, Col T. E. Typewritten carbon copy, signed, of
Lawrence's 'Diary'. 35pp, 4to, np, nd.

246 Lawrence, Col T. E. Three maps drawn by Lawrence in
ink and red and blue pencil.
    i   Northern section of Arabia showing the railway
        running through the Hedjaz. Size, 6¼ × 8 inches.
    ii Rough map of railways in Asia Minor indicating
        those open, actually in progress and proposed. Size,
        6¼ × 8 inches.
    iii Arabia and Asia Minor showing railways open, in
        progress and proposed. Size, 7 × 6 inches.

247 Lawrence, Col T. E. Autograph Manuscript, unsigned, on
Dr D. G. Hogarth and Charles Doughty. 1p, small 4to.
About 325 words. Written in ink on the verso of a
message form.

248   Lawrence, Col T. E. A collection of 10 photographs, various sizes*l* each mounted and matted. (All are concerned with the Arab Revolt; eight were taken by Lawrence and all bear manuscript notes by him.)

249   (——) Manuscript expense account, written on one side of 5 leaves, 4to. Addressed 'His Excellence Colonel Lawrence to Mohamed Abdullah Bassam, Damascus'.

250   Lawrence, Col T. E. Autograph manuscript notes, signed 'T.L.' 2pp, narrow 12mo.
These notes relate to an 'Entertainment Allowance' which Lawrence used to bribe the Arabs in the early days of the Revolt.

251   Lawrence, Col T. E. Pen and ink sketch of a plan, signed 'T. E. Lawrence'. Size 7 15/16 × 9 15/16 inches. A rough plan of attack on the Kalaat–El–Ahmar Railway station.

252   Lawrence, Col T. E. Typewritten notes on the destruction of the Fourth Turkish Army. 7pp, 4to. About 2,100 words.

253   Lawrence, Col T. E. Typewritten transcript from short-hand notes with typed signature 'T.E.L.', dictated to Edward Robinson and entitled 'The Destruction of the Fourth Army', 12pp, small 4to; about 3,500 words. Autograph Explanatory note signed 'T. E. Lawrence', attached to typescript, 1p, 12mo, np, nd. Photostat marked 'SECRET' and entitled 'The Sherif of Mecca and the Arab Movement', 5pp, folio, with the following at the end: 'General Staff War Office, 1st July, 1916'.

254   Lawrence, Col T. E. A collection of 114 photographs and 3 envelopes, each mounted on heavy white drawing paper and the whole bound into a 4to red morocco-backed volume, gilt edges.

An extremely important collection of photographs taken by Lawrence and representing an authentic commentary upon the text of *The Seven Pillars of Wisdom*. This collection was gathered together and arranged in chronological sequence by Edward Robinson.

255 Lawrence, Col T. E. Proof sheets of the official report of the Eastern Military Campaign. With maps on the verso of each leaf. 12pp, 4to.

Describes the last great push and destruction of the enemy and containing an account entitled 'The Story of the Arab Movement'.

256 Lawrence, Col T. E. A group of 8 autograph letters signed by Feisal, the third son of King Hussein, addressed to Colonel Lawrence, Mrs Mark Sykes, and to his father, the Sherif Hussein. Written in Arabic with English translations. 9pp, 12mo and 4to. (1918–19.)

257 —— Autograph pencil notes. 1p, small 4to, circa 1919. About 110 words.

These notes are somewhat incoherent but relate to the disposition of the decisions of the Arabian Congress.

258 Lawrence, Col T. E. Autograph manuscript of Feisal's speech before the Peace Conference at Paris. 3pp, small folio, Paris, 1919. About 800 words.

Lawrence's translation of the speech delivered by Feisal at the Quai d'Orsay on 6 February 1919. The copy has been annotated by Robinson: 'These speeches were a matter of collaboration between Feisal and Lawrence, with the latter usually balancing the opinions'.

259 Lawrence, Col T. E. Autograph manuscript regarding the speech delivered by Feisal, third son of Sherif Hussein, at

the Peace Conference at Paris, in 1919. 6pp, 4to. (Paris, 1919). About 1,300 words.

Annotated by Robinson as follows: 'This is a copy of a memorandum presented by Feisal, and originated and translated by Lawrence . . .'. The manuscript is corrected in Lawrence's handwriting.

260 —— Typewritten Ls. 'Feisal'. 1p, 12mo (London) 29 December, 1920. To Col T. E. Lawrence.

This letter expresses the Arab's confidence in Lawrence's ability.

261 Lawrence, Col T. E. Als 'T. E. Lawrence'. 1p, 4to, np nd. To the Bishop of Jerusalem. About 270 words.

Draft of a letter by Lawrence saying that accusations of Anti-Semitism are too silly even to deny.

262 (Lawrence, Col T. E.) Copy of a letter from Lord Stamfordham, Lord-in-Waiting to King George V, dated 17 January 1928, with a notation by Lawrence in the lower margin.

The letter is addressed to A. C. Shaw and it seems to prove that Lawrence never intended to organise an Arab uprising against the British.

263 Lawrence, Col T. E. Autograph manuscript of an essay on James Elroy Flecker, 3pp, 4to. Bound into a 4to ¼ Indian red levant morocco volume. Written in ink on one side of three leaves. About 1,500 words.

Woolley, C. Leonard & Lawrence, T. E.
Carchemish, Part I, 1914

CARCHEMISH | REPORT ON THE EXCAVATIONS AT DJERABIS | ON BEHALF OF THE BRITISH MUSEUM |

CONDUCTED BY | C. LEONARD WOOLLEY, MA |
AND T. E. LAWRENCE, MA | PART I | INTRODUC-
TORY | BY D. G. HOGARTH, MA, FBA | PRINTED BY
ORDER OF THE TRUSTEES | SOLD AT THE BRITISH
MUSEUM | (etc) 1914

p iv, Preface by G. Kenyon '. . . and Mr T. E. Lawrence who
have co-operated with Mr Hogarth in the production of this
introductory section of the report . . .'.

Carchemish, Part II, 1921

CARCHEMISH | REPORT ON THE EXCAVATIONS AT
DJERABIS | ON BEHALF OF THE BRITISH MUSEUM |
CONDUCTED BY | C. LEONARD WOOLLEY, MA |
WITH | T. E. LAWRENCE, MA, AND P. L. O. GUY |
PART II | THE TOWN DEFENCES | BY | C. L. WOOL-
LEY | PRINTED BY ORDER OF THE TRUSTEES |
SOLD AT THE BRITISH MUSEUM | AND BY MESSRS
LONGMANS & CO, 39 PATERNOSTER ROW | MR
BERNARD QUARITCH, 11 GRAFTON STREET, NEW
BOND STREET, W | AND MR HUMPHREY MILFORD,
OXFORD UNIVERSITY PRESS, AMEN CORNER |
LONDON | 1921

2Ls + 1 plate + pp (i)–xii, + pp (34)–156 + 28 plates + 23pp
of plates + 2Ls, 31½cm.

The preface states that the excavations were directed by D. G.
Hogarth, assisted by R. Campbell Thompson and T. E. Lawrence, by whom the work was continued after Hogarth's
return to England. The five following digs between 1912 and
1914 were conducted by C. L. Woolley and T. E. Lawrence.
'. . . excavations were carried on in the spring of 1920. Mr

WOOLLEY was again in charge of the work, but Mr Lawrence's services were required elsewhere . . .'

Woolley, C. Leonard and Lawrence, T. E.
The Wilderness of Zin, 1936, English Edition

THE | WILDERNESS | OF ZIN | *by* | C. LEONARD WOOLLEY | *and* | T. E. LAWRENCE | *With A Chapter on the Greek Inscriptions by* | M. N. TOD | (device) | *Introduction by* | SIR FREDERIC KENYON | JONATHAN CAPE | THIRTY BEDFORD SQUARE | LONDON

1L + p (1)–166 + 40Ls.

L 1, Half-title; verso, blank; p (1), Title; p (2), First Published by the Palestine Exploration Fund 1915 | New Edition 1936 | JONATHAN CAPE LTD, 30 BEDFORD SQUARE, LONDON | AND 91 WELLINGTON STREET, WEST, TORONTO | PRINTED IN GREAT BRITAIN IN THE CITY OF OXFORD | AT THE ALDEN PRESS | PAPER MADE BY JOHN DICKINSON & CO LTD | BOUND BY A. W. BAIN & CO LTD; pp 3–4, Contents; pp 5–8, List of illustrations; p (9), To Captain S. F. Newcombe, RE | (quotation); p (16), blank; pp 17–20, Preface | By T. E. Lawrence | ; p (21), blank; p (22), map; pp 23–161; Text; p (162), blank; 40Ls plates; versos, blank; pp 163–6, Index.

Woolley, C. Leonard, and Lawrence, T. E.
The Wilderness of Zin, 1936, American Edition

THE | WILDERNESS | OF ZIN | *by* | C. LEONARD WOOLLEY | *and* | T. E. LAWRENCE | *With an Introduction by* | SIR FREDERIC KENYON | *and a chapter on the Greek*

Inscriptions by | M. N. Tod | NEW YORK | CHARLES SCRIBNER'S SONS | 1936

1L + p (1)–166 + 40Ls.

L 1, Half-title; verso, blank; p (1), Title; p (2), First Published by the Palestine Exploration Fund 1915 | New Edition 1936 | JONATHAN CAPE LTD, 30 BEDFORD SQUARE, LONDON | AND 91 WELLINGTON STREET, WEST, TORONTO | PRINTED IN GREAT BRITAIN IN THE CITY OF OXFORD | AT THE ALDEN PRESS | PAPER MADE BY JOHN DICKINSON & CO LTD | BOUND BY A. W. BAIN & CO LTD; pp 3–4, Contents; pp 5–8, List of illustrations; p (9), To Captain S. F. Newcombe, RE | (quotation); p (10), blank; pp 11–14, Introduction; p 15, Note, C. M. Watson; p (16), blank; pp 17–20, Preface | By T. E. Lawrence; p (21), blank; p (22), map; pp 23–161, Text; p (162), blank; 40Ls plates; versos, blank; pp 163–6, Index.

Material in the Public Record Office

PRO, FO, 414/416, January 1916

A paper by Lawrence entitled 'The Politics of Mecca' which sets out his views on the Arab Revolt in no uncertain terms and this view is so important that it is quoted from at length:

. . . (Hussein's) activity seems beneficial to us, because it marches with our immediate aims, the break up of the Islamic "bloc" and the defeat and disruption of the Ottoman Empire, and because the states he would set up to succeed the Turks would be as harmless to ourselves as Turkey was before she became a tool in German hands. The Arabs are even less stable than the Turks. If properly handled they would remain in a state of political mosaic, a tissue of small jealous principalities incapable of cohesion, and yet always ready to combine against an outside force. The alternative to this seems to be the control and colonisation by a European power other than ourselves which would inevitably come into conflict with the interests we already possess in the Near East.

It is evident from this view on the Arab Revolt that Lawrence knew that any promises to the Arabs regarding a real form of independence were incompatible with Britain's interest in the Middle East, and this was a matter of concern for Lawrence who stated in *The Seven Pillars of Wisdom* that 'I could see that if we won the war the promises to the Arabs were dead paper'. The promises were, however, made and the fraud perpetrated '. . . on my conviction that Arab help was necessary to our cheap and speedy victory in the East, and that better we win and break our word than lose'. Lawrence's subsequent championing of the Arab cause at the peace settlement is considered by Knightley and Simpson to be more concerned with a desire to ensure British instead of French dominance in Syria, than a genuine sympathy for the Arab cause.

PRO, FO, 882/16, 1916

A memorandum entitled 'The Conquest of Syria if Complete' which Lawrence wrote at the beginning of 1916 and in which he set out the aims of the Arab Revolt and its tactics. The memorandum recommends the supporting of Hussein to further the Arab Revolt and suggests that the cutting of the Hedjaz railway would be the most effective tactic to adopt.

PRO, FO, 882/15, 26 March 1916

A directive from Cairo in which Lawrence's brief for putting an Arab Revolt into operation to further the British war aim is set out. The directive was published for the first time in Knightley and Simpson's *Secret Lives of Lawrence of Arabia*. It is clear from this document that the Arab Bureau regarded any Arab Revolt as a co-operative effort between the Arabs and the Allied forces with the realistic approach being that 'the most important thing of all (at all events when we are getting in touch and buying people and so on) will be cash'. Even more important, in view of subsequent events, was the statement made regarding any commitment to the Arab cause in Mesopotamia or elsewhere '. . . we do not intend to tie ourselves down to any details as to our future relations with such Arab government as is [sic] brought into existence in Irak until we have had an opportunity of seeing what the nature of that government is and how far it is in a position to carry out such assurances as it may give us. In a word for your own information, please note that we refuse to discuss with this party today any other consideration but a simple promise to do all we can to help Arab independence.' It is evident from this statement of policy that Lawrence knew, prior to the outbreak of the Arab Revolt, that no real commitment with the Arabs would be entered into.

PRO, FO, 882/13, 29 March 1916

A telegram sent on 29 March by General Robertson to the General Officer Commanding Force D, near Kut, regarding the attempt to ransom Townshend's force. The telegram makes it clear that Lawrence was empowered to negotiate for the release of Townshend's force and that a sum of £1 million was authorised to facilitate the negotiations.

PRO, FO, 882/15, 8 April 1916

A response from Lawrence to his briefing in PRO, FO, 882/15

of 26 March in which he comments on the Chief Political Officer for Mesopotamia, Sir Percy Cox, as being 'entirely ignorant of Arab Societies and of Turkish politics. . . . He does not understand our ideas but he is very open and will change his mind as required.'

PRO, FO, 882/15, 9 April 1916

An expression of Lawrence's disappointment at the absence of revolutionary fervour in Basra. In it he quotes from a letter written by Captain William Shakespear in 1915 'If the Sultan of Turkey were to disappear, The Khalifit by the consent of Islam would fall to the family of the prophet, the present representative of which is the Sherif of Mecca'. The use of this quotation would perhaps indicate where Lawrence felt the true hope for the revolt lay.

PRO, FO, 882/18, May 1916

A secret report sent by Lawrence to the War Office regarding the Khalil Pasha with whom Lawrence and Aubrey Herbert negotiated the eventual surrender of Townshend's force. In it Lawrence describes Khalil in detail and also shows a good understanding of Turkish army procedure.

PRO, FO, 882/12

The result of talks between Lawrence and Hussein on 29 July 1917 in which Hussein told Lawrence what happened between Sykes, Georges-Picot and Hussein. This information Lawrence incorporated into a report to the Arab Bureau and, although second hand, this seems to bear out Hussein's claim that he knew nothing about the Sykes-Picot agreement. In this document Lawrence said that Hussein had refused at this meeting to agree to any French annexation of Beirut and the Lebanon. 'He is extremely pleased to have trapped M. Picot into the admission that France will be satisfied in Syria with the position Great Britain desires in Iraq. That he says, means a temporary occupation of the country for strategical and political reasons. . . . In conclusion the Sherif remarked on the shortness and informality of conversations, the absence of written documents, and the fact that the only change in the situation caused by the meeting was the French renunciation of the ideas of annexation, permanent occupation, or suzerainty of any part of Syria.' Although Lawrence states in *The Seven Pillars of Wisdom*, 'I had early betrayed the [Sykes-Picot] treaty's existence to Feisal', it is evident that he had not told him the full terms of the treaty and this may have been because the Arab Bureau were trying to undermine the treaty, not because of any betrayal of the Arabs but because the French were gaining a base in the Middle East. Hussein's misunderstanding of the Sykes-Picot treaty worried Lieutenant Colonel C. E. Wilson who wrote to Wingate on 31 July 1917 concerning the troubles that this would give rise to in the wake of the fall of Damascus.

Section C
Works about T. E. Lawrence

Aldington, Richard
Lawrence of Arabia, 1955

LAWRENCE | OF | ARABIA | *A Biographical Enquiry* | *by* |
RICHARD   ALDINGTON | (Quotation) | *COLLINS* | *ST*
JAMES'S PLACE, LONDON | *1955*

pp (1)–448, illus, maps, 21cm.

p (1), Half-title; verso, blank; frontispiece; p (3), Title-page;
verso, printing details; p (5), Dedication; verso, blank; pp (7)–
(8), List of Contents; p (9), List of Illustrations; p (10), List of
maps; pp 11–14, Introductory letter to Alister Kershaw; p 15,
Part one; verso, blank; pp 17–388, Text; pp (389)–(391), Maps;
pp 392–420, List of sources; pp 421–5, Bibliography; p 426,
Acknowledgements; pp 427–48, Index.

This work by Aldington is severely critical of Lawrence and on
its publication received several favourable reviews but many more
which were unfavourable. It did, however, raise doubts concerning Lawrence which perhaps influenced later biographers. At the
same time, it is by no means certain that Aldington's conclusions
are completely accurate in view of the denials and counterclaims
that appeared in periodical articles after its publication.

Regardless of the conclusions that one reaches regarding
Aldington's work, it must be accepted that this is an important
work in the study of Lawrence. Aldington opened the way to a
reappraisal of 'the Lawrence legend' and this probably inspired
a fresh and more critical examination of Lawrence's public and
private life.

Aldridge, James
'Heroes of the empty view', by James Aldridge
London: The Bodley Head, 1954

400pp, 21½cm.

A novel based on the exploits of Lawrence but in a contemporary setting.

Altounyan, E. H. R.
'Ornament of Honour', by E. H. R. Altounyan
London: CUP, 1937

(vi), 131pp, 21½cm.

A poem dedicated to Lawrence.

Armitage, Flora
The Desert and the Stars, 1956

The Desert and the Stars | *A PORTRAIT OF T. E. LAW-RENCE* | *by* | FLORA ARMITAGE | (rule) | FABER AND FABER | 24 Russell Square | London |

1L + pp 3–334 + 1L.

L 1, blank; p (3), Half-title; verso, blank; Frontispiece; p 5, Title-page; verso, *First published in England in mcmlvi* | *by Faber and Faber Limited* | *24 Russell Square, London, WC1* | *Printed in Great Britain by* | *Western Printing Services, Limited, Bristol* | *All rights reserved* | p 7, Contents; verso, blank; p 9, Quotation from the Ancient Mariner; p (10), blank; pp 11–(12), Acknowledgements; pp 13–323, Text; pp 324–7, Bibliography; p (328), blank; pp 329–34, Index; + 1L, blank.

This work is a straightforward account of Lawrence's life, with a section (pp 302–23) which refutes all the criticism made by Aldington in his work on Lawrence (see p 83).

Baxter, Frank Condie
'An Annotated Check List of a Collection of Writings by and About T. E. Lawrence', by Frank Condie Baxter
Los Angeles: 1968

(only 60 copies printed).

Blackmur, R. P.
The Expense of Greatness, by R. P. Blackmur
Gloucester, Mass: Peter Smith, 1958

305pp, 21cm.

The essay on Lawrence 'The everlasting effort: A citation of T. E. Lawrence' appears on pp 1–36. It is a critical study of Lawrence as a writer and concludes: 'When we say that Lawrence never produced a character, not even his own, if we add that he produced nevertheless almost everything that makes for character, we have said very nearly what is necessary. It was his everlasting effort.'

Broughton, Harry
Lawrence of Arabia and Wareham, nd

LAWRENCE OF ARABIA | AND WAREHAM | COM-PILED BY HARRY BROUGHTON | (*Sometime Mayor of Wareham*) | (device) | PICTORIAL MUSEUM, WARE-HAM, DORSET

4 unpaginated leaves.

L 1, Title; verso, illustrations; L 2, Text; verso, map; L 3, map; verso, illustrations; L 4, text; verso, text.

A very brief guide to Lawrence's associations with Wareham. Subsequent editions were published under the title 'Lawrence of Arabia and Dorset' with no change in format.

Burton, Percy
'Adventures among Immortals', by Percy Burton
London: Hutchinson & Co, 1938

256pp, illus, index, 21cm.

This is the biography of a showman, Percy Burton, as told to Lowell Thomas. Its interest lies in the fact that Burton was responsible for Lowell Thomas' lecture tour of Britain. The section on Lawrence is on pp 204–8 and includes a letter from Lawrence regarding an offer from Lord Northcliffe concerning an interview in *The Times*. Lawrence refused to allow Burton to interview him for *The Times* because 'I never care what people say of me, or about me, but I try not to help them to do it, and I will not do it myself'.

Caudwell, Christopher (pseud)
'Studies in a Dying Culture', by Christopher Caudwell, with an introduction by John Strachey
London: Bodley Head, 1938

xxv, 228pp, 19cm.

The section on Lawrence appears between pp 20–43. This is a very interesting work, presenting as it does a communist view of Lawrence. It is also a study in heroism, Caudwell's theme being that the bourgeois society could only produce 'a might-have-been, the pathetic figure of T. E. Lawrence'.

Christopher Caudwell is a pseudonym for C. H. J. Sprigg.

Churchill, Winston Spencer
'Great Contemporaries', by Winston Spencer Churchill
London: Thornton Butterworth, 1937

335pp, illus, index, 21cm.

The section on Lawrence, with a portrait, appears between pp 155 and 167. The majority of this work on Lawrence was first published in *T. E. Lawrence by his friends* (see p 104).

Clark, Ronald H.
'Brough Superior: the Rolls-Royce of Motor Cycles', by Ronald H. Clark
Norwich: Goose & Son, 1964

pp (i)–xviii, pp 1–174, 22cm.

References to Lawrence: pp 117–25, 141.

Includes a reproduction of a letter to Brough from Lawrence dated 27 January 1931 and a picture of Lawrence on his motor bike together with the maker.

'Country Life' Limited, 1964
'Clouds Hill, Dorset, 1964'

CLOUDS HILL | DORSET | 1964 | THE NATIONAL TRUST | LONDON | Country Life Limited |

pp 1–19.

p 1, Title; pp 2–19, Text.

This is a booklet issued by the National Trust, which looks

after Lawrence's Dorset home. It is divided into three main parts:

1 T. E. Lawrence of Arabia and Clouds Hill, by B. H. Liddell Hart (pp 2–11).
2 Lawrence and Clouds Hill, by A. W. Lawrence (pp 12–14).
3 The Cottage.

It is a useful work, as it gives a brief outline of Lawrence's life, his association with Clouds Hill and detail as to the material and books with which he surrounded himself in his cottage.

Duval, Elizabeth W.
'T. E. Lawrence: A Bibliography', 1938

T. E. LAWRENCE | A BIBLIOGRAPHY | BY ELIZA-BETH W. DUVAL | ARROW EDITIONS, NEW YORK

1L + pp (1)–96 + 1L.

L 1, blank; p (1), Title-page; verso, blank; p (3), List of Contents; verso, blank; pp 5–6, Foreword; pp (7)–93, Text; pp 94–5, Index; p (96), blank; L 2, blank.

This is the only major bibliographical work which has appeared on Lawrence and is, of course, only useful for material published before 1938. The work is arranged in the following manner:

Works by T. E. Lawrence, J. H. Ross, 'T. E. Lawrence', T. E. Shaw.
Introductions and prefatory letters.
Contributions to periodicals and newspapers.
Miscellanea.
Letters by Lawrence.
Addenda.

The entries are rarely annotated, except with regard to some of the letters to the press, where indication as to content is given.

Edmonds, Charles
'T. E. Lawrence', 1935

T. E. LAWRENCE | BY | CHARLES EDMONDS | AUTHOR OF 'A SUBALTERN'S WAR' | (QUOTA-TION) | PETER DAVIES LIMITED | 1935

pp (1)–192.

p (1), Half-title; verso, blank; frontispiece; p (3), Title-page; p (4), *First published in November* 1935 etc; pp 5–6, Preface; p 7, Contents and maps; p 8, Dates in Lawrence's life; pp 9–189, Text; p 190, Bibliographical note; pp 191–2, Index.

A relatively straightforward biography of Lawrence based on the facts as put forward by Lawrence, and the popular conception of Lawrence's life.

Charles Edmonds is a pseudonym for Charles Edmund Carrington.

Faisal I, King of Iraq
Letters of King Faisal to Colonel Lawrence

pp (1)–(20), 25cm.

Letter 1, two pages long, headed:
    Letter from His Majesty King Feisul to | Colonel Lawrence
        (undated)
Letter 2, six pages long, headed:
    Letter from His Majesty King Feisul to | Colonel Lawrence
        (undated)

Letter 3, two pages long, headed:
> Letter from His Majesty King Feisul to | Colonel Lawrence
> (dated 6 October 1921)

This collection has no title-page and is completely in typescript, with typing on one side of the page only. There is no indication of translation or source and each letter is headed *'COPY'*.

This copy is BM 10922 g 10.

G

'Annotations on some Minor Writings of T. E. Lawrence', 1935

Annotations | on | Some Minor Writings | of | 'T. E. Lawrence' | by | G | Eric Partridge, Ltd | at the Scholartis Press | Thirty Museum Street, London | 1935

1L + pp (iii)–x, + pp 11–28.

1L, blank; p (iii), Half-title; verso, This Edition is limited to | Five hundred copies of which | Four hundred and fifty are | for sale. Copy No 45; frontispiece (line drawing of Lawrence by Frederick Carter, ARE, previously unpublished); p (v), Title-page; verso, Printed and made in Great Britain by | W. Graves, 8/10 Stanhope Street, London, NW1; p vii, Prefatory note; verso, blank; pp ix–x, Index to the minor writings; pp 11–28, Text.

Contents Note
I   Editiones Principes | Some Essays, Translations, Letters, etc, pp 11–16.
II Editiones Principes | Some Forewords, pp 17–20.
III Editiones Principes | Some contributions, pp 21–3.
IV Obiter Scripta | Some Extracts from Letters, pp 24–8.
'G' is Terence Fytton Armstrong.

German-Reed, T.
'Bibliographical Notes on T. E. Lawrence's "Seven Pillars of Wisdom" and "Revolt in the Desert",' nd

BIBLIOGRAPHICAL NOTES | ON | T. E. LAWRENCE'S | *SEVEN PILLARS OF WISDOM* | AND | *REVOLT IN THE DESERT* | BY T. GERMAN-REED | (Decoration) | LONDON MCMXXVIII | W. & G. FOYLE LIMITED | CHARING CROSS ROAD, WC2

1L + (vi) + pp 1–16 + 2Ls.

L 1, blank; p (i), Half-title; verso, This Edition is limited to Three hundred and | seventy-five copies of which Three hundred | and fifty are for sale. This is No 142. | The Decoration is from | a Wood Engraving by | Paul Nash; p (iii), Title-page; verso, blank; p (v), Dedication; p (vi), blank; pp 1–16, Text; L 2, Printed by etc; L 3, blank.

The author starts by describing the circumstances surrounding the publication of *The Seven Pillars of Wisdom* and *Revolt in the Desert*. Detailed bibliographical differences between the 'Incomplete' and 'Complete' copies of *Seven Pillars* are discussed, together with information regarding the printers and the binders. Similar detail is also given for *Revolt in the Desert*. Pages 12–16 have bibliographical descriptions of the various editions of the two works. This work has, however, been criticised for its omission of the Oxford edition of *Seven Pillars* (see article by T. P. Greig, p 138).

Glen, Douglas
'In the Steps of Lawrence of Arabia', 1939

IN THE STEPS OF | LAWRENCE OF ARABIA | *By* | DOUGLAS GLEN | (device) | LONDON | RICH & COWAN, LTD | 37 BEDFORD SQUARE, WCI

p (iii)–(vi) + 11–320.

p (iii), Title; p (iv), MADE IN GREAT BRITAIN | PRINTED AND BOUND BY PURNELL AND SONS, LTD, PAULTON (SOMERSET) AND LONDON, | FOR MESSRS RICH AND COWAN, LIMITED, 37 BEDFORD SQUARE, LONDON, WCI | ON PAPER SUPPLIED BY W. D. HORROCKS AND SONS LTD; pp v–vi, Contents; pp 11–317, Text; pp 318–20, Index.

This work about Lawrence was written as a result of 'a pilgrimage' by the author, who traced Lawrence's movements in the Middle East. The journey was made in 1938, and the text consists of the author's observations interspersed by Lawrence's descriptions of events.

Golding, Louis
'In the Steps of Moses the Conqueror', by Louis Golding
London: Rich & Cowan Ltd, 1938

viii, 426pp, illus, map, index.

This journey was made by Golding to retrace the route of Moses and the Israelites to the Promised Land. In undertaking this journey he visited many of the places which figured in Lawrence's life in Arabia and this motivated a consideration of Lawrence's part in the Arab Revolt. This book also includes

Lawrence's 'Confession of Faith' (pp 146–7), which was a series of pencil scribblings found amongst his papers after his death.

Gorman, Major J. T.
'With Lawrence to Damascus', 1940

GREAT EXPLOITS | WITH LAWRENCE | TO DAMAS-CUS | *By* | MAJOR J. T. GORMAN | (Device) | OXFORD UNIVERSITY PRESS | LONDON. NEW YORK. TORONTO

pp (i)–(iv), 1–44.

p (i), Half-title; p (ii), Frontispiece, p (iii), Title; p (iv), PRINTED 1940 IN GREAT BRITAIN BY RICHARD CLAY AND COMPANY, LTD, | BUNGAY, SUFFOLK; pp (1)–44, Text.

A very brief account of the Arab Revolt and its effects, but based on the romantic conception of the Lawrence legend.

Graves, Robert
'Lawrence and the Arabs', 1927

LAWRENCE AND THE | ARABS | *By* | ROBERT GRAVES | (device) | ILLUSTRATIONS EDITED BY | ERIC KENNINGTON | MAPS BY | HERRY PERRY | LONDON | JONATHAN CAPE 30 BEDFORD SQUARE

1L + pp 1–454.

1L, Half-title; verso, quotation; frontispiece; p (1), Title-page; verso, First Published in mcmxxvii etc; pp 3–4, List of illustrations; pp 5–7, Introduction; p (8), blank; p (9), Half-title; p (10), blank; pp 11–437, Text; pp 438–48, appendices; pp 449–54, index.

This biography was one of the two authorised by Lawrence, the other being by Liddell Hart (see p 95). The Graves work was preceded by the biography by Lowell Thomas, which appeared in 1925 (see p 119) and is described by Graves as being 'an inaccurate and sentimental account of Lawrence'. Graves' work must be examined in the light of subsequent material and with the reservation that it relied very heavily on *The Seven Pillars of Wisdom* and information supplied by Lawrence (see also T. E. Lawrence: *To his biographers Robert Graves and Liddell Hart* on p 53).

Graves maintained that he had attempted a critical study of Lawrence and 'the popular verdict that he is the most remarkable living Englishman, though I dislike such verdicts, I am inclined to accept'. His book also accepts Lawrence's account of the Deraa incident, and many of the other events which have since caused controversy were accepted at face value by Graves. Regarding the identity of the S.A. to whom *Seven Pillars* is dedicated, Graves favoured Farida el Akl as the person to whom this cipher referred (Lawrence's Arabic teacher at Jebail, in Syria, before the war) but this identification of S.A. has never been satisfactorily resolved although Knightley and Simpson believe that S.A. was in fact Dahoum whose proper name was Salim Ahmed. In his work on Lawrence, Villars states that Graves, when pursuing the mystery with Lawrence, had been further misled and points out 'As for Robert Graves, Lawrence seems to have taken an evil delight in misleading him' (p 305). Despite this, Graves' book is an important biography of Lawrence and an extremely readable account although it does not, and probably could not at that time, provide answers to some of the mystery surrounding Lawrence.

Halifax, The Viscount
'T. E. Lawrence: An address delivered at St Paul's
Cathedral', Wednesday, 29 January 1936
London: OUP, 1936

This is a copy of the address delivered at the memorial service held for Lawrence.

Hart, B. H. Liddell
'T. E. Lawrence in Arabia and After', 1965

LIDDELL HART | 'T. E. Lawrence' | in Arabia and after | JONATHAN CAPE | THIRTY BEDFORD SQUARE LONDON

1L + pp (1)–(490) + 2Ls, 20cm.

L 1, Half-title; verso, blank; p (1), Title-page; verso, First Published 1934 etc; pp 3–4, List of Contents and maps; p (5), Dedication; verso, blank; pp 7–9, Preface; p 9, Special note for military readers; p 10, Special note for civilian readers; p (11), Book one, Personal Prologue; verso, blank; pp 13–482, Text; pp 483–9, Index; p (490), Map; + 2Ls, Maps.

This work, originally published in 1934, was initially conceived as a study of the war in the Middle East from the military viewpoint, though Lawrence would inevitably have been considered. In his introduction, Liddell Hart states that he felt this examination would tend to bring Lawrence's activities into their true perspective but his conclusion was that 'But for him the Arab Revolt would have remained a collection of slight and passing incidents'. Liddell Hart's main interest is, therefore, in the military aspect of Lawrence's life and he feels that his understanding of the war, and the tactics that he evolved, were far superior to many of the regular army officers, although Liddell Hart does not over-emphasise the importance of the Arab Revolt in the war as a whole. (See also the article by Liddell Hart, p 140.)

Houston, Guyla Bond
Thomas Edward Lawrence, 1888–1935. A checklist of Lawrenciana, 1915–65
Stillwater Oklahoma: 1967

ff 148, 29cm (Typewritten).

Covers works by and about Lawrence including periodical articles and lists the various editions of each publication. The entries are not annotated. The work is also available on microfilm from the Imperial War Museum.

Howard, Michael S.
'Jonathan Cape, Publisher', 1971

Jonathan Cape | Publisher | HERBERT JONATHAN CAPE | G. WREN HOWARD | (Rule) | *Michael S. Howard* | (Device) | JONATHAN CAPE | THIRTY BEDFORD SQUARE, LONDON

pp 352, illus, 24cm.

p (1), Reproduction of first letterhead of Jonathan Cape, Publisher; verso, blank; p (3), Title-page; verso, First published 1971 etc; p (5), Contents; verso, blank; pp 7–9, List of illustrations; p (10), blank; pp 11–15, Preface; p (16), blank; pp (17)–333, Text; p (334), blank; pp 335–51, Index; p (352), blank.

References to Lawrence: pp 50, 81, 96, 109, 158, 168; and Arabia Deserta, 26–9; 'Key to our success', 82 and *Seven Pillars*, 82–7; 89–94, 143, 151–5; translation work, 86, 88–9; *Revolt* abridgement of *Seven Pillars*, 90–4, 144–5; and *Mint*, 147–9, 213–14; death, 154.

This work, written by the past chairman of Jonathan Cape, is of great value in any consideration of the work of Lawrence, presenting, as it does, the publisher's side of the events surrounding the publication of *The Seven Pillars of Wisdom*, *Revolt in the Desert* and *The Mint*. The book makes it plain that Lawrence's work was instrumental in ensuring the success of the firm, and Wren Howard declared, 'Always from the very beginning, Lawrence was the key to our success'. This is illustrated by the fact that *Revolt in the Desert* largely accounted for a rise in Cape's sales in 1927 of 150 per cent. The book reproduces the correspondence between Lawrence and Jonathan Cape, and the draft agreement for *Revolt in the Desert*, which was heavily amended by Bernard Shaw. Jonathan Cape had hoped that Lawrence would join the firm in an editorial capacity and in his contribution to *T. E. Lawrence by his Friends* he wrote: 'He enjoyed the fascination of unknown manuscripts, and the adventure of discovery; and he relished the practical delights of dealing with type, paper and binding'. In fact Lawrence did undertake some translation work for Cape but even in this field his criticism of his own work was paramount, and when translating Sturly he abandoned the work and destroyed his manuscript, returning the cheque to Jonathan Cape who refused to accept it. Lawrence wrote to Cape on 21 February 1924: 'You should have kept my cheque, and added one of yours to it, and had a first-rate version done by a real proper writer'. This reaction from Lawrence prompted Wren Howard to write: 'This wretched man had better write a novel. It wd help to clear his addled head' (annotation to Lawrence's letter).

The publication of *The Seven Pillars of Wisdom* was first broached by Lawrence in 1922 after Garnett had produced an abridgement of the 'Oxford Text'. The abridgement interested Bernard Shaw who approached Constable with a view to its publication, and this prompted Garnett to write to Lawrence asking if he wanted Cape to be made aware of the abridgement. Lawrence replied that Garnett could mention the book to Cape but he was concerned at the cost of production in view of Cape's resources, 'Of course I'd be very glad if he got it: but it seems to me a speculation unjustifiably large for his resources. The thing may be a complete frost, and will cost £3,000 to produce: and I reckon that would about bust him.' (In fact the book cost £13,000 to produce.) This concern was expressed again by Lawrence in a letter to Jonathan Cape in the late December of 1922 when he wrote: '. . . let me warn you again that the selling of it is a chance, and I'd be very sorry (but quite helpless) if it did you in. To tackle so speculative and so large a book seems to me doubtful business for so new a firm . . . and it's my private opinion that the book isn't very good.'

The Seven Pillars appeared as a subscribers' edition in 1926, and it was the expense of this edition which led to the publication of the abridgement, *Revolt in the Desert*, in 1927. By June over 30,000 copies had been sold, which caused Lawrence to draft an instruction to withdraw the book as this was the number that he had calculated as necessary to clear his debts. At the time of the book's withdrawal it had sold 90,000 copies and contributed to a gigantic leap forward in Cape's profits from around £2,000 to nearly £28,000. This, according to Howard, was an embarrassment as 'the Inland Revenue became excited, and required a long and cogent memorandum to explain this sudden opulence'. After Lawrence's death, Cape proposed to reprint *Revolt in the Desert* as he regarded the embargo as valid only whilst Lawrence was alive. The reprint was stopped by A. W.

Lawrence who held that Lawrence's wishes should be observed and that if Cape went ahead with publication he would not be the publisher of a trade edition of *The Seven Pillars of Wisdom*. As a result, the reprint was cancelled and the rights to publish *Seven Pillars* negotiated, which included an agreement not to reprint *Revolt in the Desert* for a further thirty years. *Seven Pillars* was published on 29 July 1935 with a limited edition of 750 numbered copies printed on pure rag paper and 30,000 for general sale, a number which had to be doubled before publication; by December 1935 100,000 copies had been sold.

The Mint was also published by Cape in 1955 but this was not the first publication as fifty copies had been published by Doubleday in 1935 to secure American copyright. The book was issued in two editions, a limited unexpurgated edition, and a standard edition with gaps showing the removal of offending words. The text had in fact been set up in 1947 but publication was delayed to avoid offence to the officer 'whose portrait Lawrence drew, devastatingly, in Chapter 20 of *The Mint*'.

This work is extremely valuable for the information that it gives about the publication of Lawrence's important works both from the publisher's side and from their dealings with Lawrence. It is a very readable book giving a further insight into Lawrence and also the rise of the publishing house of Jonathan Cape.

Kiernan, R. H.
'Lawrence of Arabia', 1935

LAWRENCE OF | ARABIA | *By* | R. H. KIERNAN | AUTHOR OF | 'LLOYD GEORGE',' BADEN-POWELL' | ETC | *With Maps and Illustrations* | (Device) | GEORGE G. HARRAP & CO LTD | LONDON TORONTO BOMBAY SYDNEY pp (i)–(viii), 11–196.

1L, blank; p (iii), Title-page; p (iv), Dedication; pp (v)–(vi), Introduction; p (vii), Contents; p (viii), Maps and Illustrations; pp 11–186, Text; pp 187–95, Appendices; p 196, Bibliography.

A readable account of Lawrence's life mainly concerning his Arabian exploits, but the book lacks any real depth.

Kiernan, R. H.
'The Unveiling of Arabia', by R. H. Kiernan
London: Harrap & Co, 1937

360pp, illus, maps, bibl, index, 22cm.

References to Lawrence: pp 119–20, 149, 151, 174, 242, 288, 292, 295, 302–3, 317.

This work deals mainly with the European exploration of Arabia and it is in this connection that Lawrence is considered with a section dealing with his mapping work carried out prior to the Arab Revolt.

Knight, G. Wilson
'Neglected Powers: Essays on Nineteenth and Twentieth Century Literature', by G. Wilson Knight
London: Routledge & Kegan Paul, 1971

515pp, app, indexes, 22cm.

Essay on Lawrence: pp 309–51.

This essay aims at dealing with the nature of Lawrence's impact which the author considers to be remarkable in view of the faults attributed to Lawrence by his detractors, which even included Lawrence. Professor Wilson Knight begins by comparing Lawrence with Byron through their background, personalities, physical limitations and homosexual tendencies. The essay continues by discussing the Arab Revolt and the self-examination which Lawrence made of his actions and his motives and especially his regret at his entanglement in the Arab Revolt.

In discussing Lawrence's homosexual tendencies, Wilson Knight again draws parallels with Byron, comparing Lawrence's friendship with Farraj and Daud with that of Byron for Nicola Giraud in Athens. The essay then continues by producing extracts from *T. E. Lawrence by his Friends* to provide a picture of him by the people that really knew the man. It ends by examining Lawrence's period in the RAF and concludes that it served 'his secret impulse to degradation coming openly and creatively into play' and also because in the Air Force he had placed himself 'in precisely the most important spot, nationally speaking, that was open to him'. Wilson Knight's conclusion is that Lawrence realised the potential that the Air Force had and the part that it was to play in the future. 'In putting aside all obvious temptation to present fame and glamour, Lawrence was, in fact, quietly, and in his own unique and prescient way, devoting himself to victory in the Battle of Britain.'

Knightley, Phillip and Simpson, Colin
'The Secret Lives of Lawrence of Arabia', 1969

The Secret Lives of | LAWRENCE | OF ARABIA | *Phillip Knightley and Colin Simpson* | Nelson

x + pp (1)–293.

p (i), Half-title; verso, blank; p (iii), Title-page; p (iv), Thomas

Nelson & Sons Ltd etc; p (v), Contents; p (vi), Plates; p (vii), Copyright Acknowledgements; pp (viii)–ix, Acknowledgements; p (x), Quotation; pp (1)–6, Introduction; pp (7)–276, Text; pp (277)–278, Bibliography; pp (279)–93, Index; + 1 blank page.

This is an important book because of its recent publication but even more because of its source material. The authors were allowed access by the trustees to the Lawrence manuscripts in the Bodleian Library, closed to public scrutiny until the year AD 2000. The collection is mainly in bound form and listed for the library's use, but is not catalogued or indexed as such.

The work divides Lawrence's life into four main parts. The first part covers his training period as a secret agent while posing as an archaeologist in Asia Minor; the second part is considered to be the practical application of that training during the Arab Revolt; the third is designated as the period when he was trying to fade into the obscurity of service life; and the final part his friendship with the Shaws. The authors also deal at some length with Lawrence's torture at Deraa and the effect that this had upon his emotional life after the war. This aspect of Lawrence's life was ignored or at best glossed over in earlier biographies with the exception of the work by Aldington.

The Lawrence legend is examined in the light of the age in which he lived and the authors conclude that it was created because the desert war had a romantic air when compared with the battlefields of Europe. They suggest that his importance 'lies in the fact that he was not only . . . representative of his time and his class, but also of the policy and the tactics adopted by an imperial power to protect its interests'.

This work is most interesting because of its contemporary evaluation of Lawrence and because of the new material from the Bodleian Library and the Public Records Office. It has succeeded in solving some of the unanswered questions about Lawrence and in explaining some of the legend, especially that part which dealt with his original involvement in the Arab Revolt and the subsequent betrayal of promises to the Arabs. In the light of this new material and the conclusions that can be drawn, however, it does seem that the definitive biography of Lawrence has still to be written. (This work originally appeared as a series of articles in the *Sunday Times* during June 1968.)

Lawrence, Arnold Walter
'Letters to T. E. Lawrence', 1962

LETTERS | to | T. E. LAWRENCE | Edited by | A. W. LAWRENCE | (device) | LONDON | JONATHAN CAPE 30 BEDFORD SQUARE

pp (1)–216 + 1L.

p (1), Half-title; verso, blank; p (3), Title-page; verso, First Published 1962 etc; p (5)–(6), Contents; p (7)–(8), Preface; p (9), Half-title; p (10), Editor's note; pp 11–214, Text; pp 215–16, Index; + 1L, blank.

The text of the letters has been reproduced exactly, apart from corrections of spelling and punctuation. Some omissions have been made and these are indicated by (. . . omitted). Reference has been made to Lawrence's side where it has been published, mainly from Garnett's 1938 edition of *The Letters of T. E. Lawrence*. The style of reference used is the initials D.G. followed by the number assigned to each letter in the book, not the page number. The text is arranged alphabetically by the writers, which makes for ease of use if the reader is interested in the correspondence between Lawrence and a particular correspondent such as David Garnett. This is a useful work although, to gain full value from it, one needs to be able to consult Lawrence's side of the correspondence.

The editorial matter is printed in italic type and where it impinges on the text it is also enclosed by square brackets.

A. W. Lawrence's reasons for publishing this selection of letters was to correct the inadequate or mistaken portrayals of his brother in books and on the stage. He also felt that if he was made the subject of a film 'the limitations of the medium will, at the best, entail an extreme simplification of the character'. The letters are printed to throw light on the recipient.

Lawrence, Arnold Walter
'T. E. Lawrence by His Friends', 1937

T. E. LAWRENCE | BY HIS FRIENDS | EDITED BY | A. W. LAWRENCE | (device) | JONATHAN CAPE | THIRTY BEDFORD SQUARE | LONDON

pp (1)–595, 23cm.

p (1), Half-title; verso, blank; Frontispiece; p (3), Title-page; verso, First published 1937 etc; pp 5–6, Preface; pp 7–10, List of Contents; p 11, List of Illustrations; verso, blank; p 13, Dates in the life of T. E. Lawrence; verso, blank; pp 16–595, Text.

This collection consists of a series of impressions by people who knew Lawrence personally and who were invited to write objectively about that aspect of him which they knew best.

Contents Note

Introductory Section	Manhood
Home	The War: His Comrades
The Boy and the Man	The War: In action
The East: Ancient and Modern	The War and after

Publicity	Royal Air Force: India
Eastern Politics	Later general views
Post-war general views	Literature
Personal Crisis	Music
Oxford and London	Later Friendships
The Ranks: Royal Air Force	Motor Bicycling
Royal Tank Corps	Speed boats
Book Production	Editor's Postscript
A Business Footing	

The sections on Literature and Music each contain catalogues of the collections in Lawrence's cottage at Clouds Hill, Dorset, (see also T. E. Lawrence, *Minorities*, p 39).

Lönnroth, Eric
'Lawrence of Arabia', 1956

ERIC LÖNNROTH | LAWRENCE | *Of* | ARABIA | AN HISTORICAL APPRECIATION | (device) | VALLENTINE, MITCHELL. LONDON

1L + pp (i)–xviii + 1–102pp + 1L.

L 1, blank; p (i), Half-title; verso, blank; p (iii), Title-page; p (iv), *First published in Sweden by Albert Bonnier* | *First published in English 1956* | *by Vallentine Mitchell & Co Ltd* | *All rights reserved* | Translated from the Swedish by Ruth Lewis | *Set in 12 on 14pt Bookprint by The Sharon Press, and printed in Great Britain by The Alcuin Press, Welwyn Garden City, Herts*; p v, Contents; p vi, Map of the Middle East in 1917; pp vii–viii, Foreword; pp ix–xviii, Introduction; pp 1–98, Text; p 99, Turkish cartoon on Lawrence's death; pp 100–2, Index; L 2, blank.

The work is based on the material available when it was published in Swedish in 1943. The English edition was only revised on points of detail and did not take into account material published since that date. It is valuable in that it presents a view of Lawrence by an outsider unmoved by any emotive connections with the Arab Revolt, though it is not a highly penetrative study. The introduction by the author presents a brief but useful review of the major works about Lawrence which had appeared, and details their bias.

Macphail, Andrew
'Three Persons', by Sir Andrew Macphail
London: John Murray, 1929

xi, 240pp, illus, index, 22cm.

References to Lawrence, with a portrait, pp 193–235.

The section on Lawrence is in two parts: the first deals with the myth as created by Lowell Thomas and the second 'The Truth', an assessment of Lawrence's military position and importance.

Marsh, Edward
'A Number of People: A Book of Reminiscences', by Edward Marsh
London: Heinemann, 1939

xii, 420pp, illus, index, 21½cm.

The references to Lawrence are on pp 234–9 and 344–5. This work is of little importance. It reproduces three letters which appear in David Garnett's *Letters* (see p 34) introduced by a brief mention of the author's friendship with Lawrence.

Namier, L. B.
'In the Margin of History', by L. B. Namier
London: Macmillan, 1939

viii, 304pp, 20cm.

The section on Lawrence falls on pp 273–304 and consists of reprints of three essays on Lawrence which appeared first in the *Manchester Guardian* in 1935 and 1939.

The first essay, entitled 'Lawrence as I knew him', was written on the day of Lawrence's death and appeared in the *Manchester Guardian* of 20 May 1935. Although Namier knew Lawrence as an undergraduate, the essay deals mainly with the period Lawrence spent at All Souls in 1920 and subsequently when Namier was Political Secretary to the Jewish Agency for Palestine. It deals with Lawrence's desire to escape from the public eye with, at the same time, a desire to be seen and recognised. It also deals with Lawrence's tastes in reading and art and other aspects of him as a man. In considering the position of Lawrence with regard to Zionism, he was thought by Namier to be pro-Zionist and was even prepared to testify on behalf of Zionism to the Cabinet. 'I repeated the offer at the time to Mr Malcolm MacDonald, but nothing came of it.'

The essay continues with a consideration of the Cairo Conference of 1921 and the separation of Transjordan from Palestine. According to Lawrence, the original decision was for Transjordan and Palestine to be one but, as the conference was considering the point, Abdulla was marching from Hedjaz to Transjordan to attack the French in Syria. It was decided to negotiate with him with only three alternatives, one of which involved the use of British troops, the second a French presence and the third, which was the one adopted, the establishment of a native state under British control. The essay also includes snippets of conversation between Namier and Lawrence on the policing in Palestine, the Revolt in Mesopotamia and Ibn Saud.

The second essay is entitled 'Seven Pillars of Wisdom' and this appeared in the *Manchester Guardian* of 29 July 1935. Namier considers it to be a difficult book to write about as 'a mind and life break through the pages of the book with a stark directness such as few writers would dare, or be able, to achieve'. He considers Lawrence's involvement with pain which turned him into an ascetic, and it was through the conditions that he endured in the desert that 'he broke through the fetters and became a spirit let adrift'. In considering the book from the literary aspect Namier feels that ' "The Seven Pillars", written in a style and imagery seldom surpassed or even equalled, will live as a work of art, far greater than Lawrence's material achievements'. Namier illustrates this by quotations from the book, beginning with his geographical descriptions of Arab towns and concluding with Lawrence's evocative description of a battlefield strewn with Turkish dead.

The third essay is entitled 'His Letters' and this appeared in the *Manchester Guardian* for 7 January 1939. In this review of *The Letters of T. E. Lawrence* edited by Garnett, he begins by stating the problem of trying to review a book in which the whole of Lawrence's life can be traced through his letters. The problem is heightened by the fact that Lawrence rarely wrote informative letters because he considered 'letter-writing is a vice', and consequently his letters were discourses rather than informative. This review concentrates on one psychological aspect of Lawrence's letters, his 'pursuit of an indefinable disbodied self and its direct expression divorced from matter, and of its depressing counterpart in his enlisting as a private'.

This pursuit was expressed through a yearning for the peace of empty spaces and in a letter he wrote in 1908 he described a plain as '. . . the best country: the purifying influence is the paramount one in a plain . . . one feels the littleness of things, of details, and the great and unbroken level of peacefulness of the whole . . .', or in 1922 when he wrote '. . . the Arab East to me is always an empty place . . .' Lawrence believed that poetry was the only essential branch of letters and his prose writing was only because he could not write poetry '. . . so in prose I aimed at providing a meal for the fellow-seekers with myself'.

In considering Lawrence's enlistment, Namier concludes that none of the explanations that he gave were wholly satisfactory and he knew this as he wrote in 1922, 'All these are reasons: but unless they are cumulative they are miserably inadequate. I wanted to join up, that's all . . .' He is certain, however, that the often quoted reason of doing penance for letting down the Arabs has no substance in fact as Lawrence felt that Britain had kept her promises as far as the British spheres of influence were concerned. To substantiate this he quotes from Lawrence's draft preface to *The Seven Pillars of Wisdom*, dated 18 November 1922, in which he discussed Winston Churchill's settlement as follows: 'He executed the whole McMahon undertaking (called a treaty by some who have not seen it) for Palestine, for Trans-jordania, and for Arabia. In Mesopotamia he went far beyond its provisions . . . I do not wish . . . to make long explanations: but must put on record my conviction that England is out of the Arab affair with clean hands.' This view was further expressed in a letter to Professor Yale dated 22 October 1929 which stated that Churchill's settlement was an honourable one and '. . . so pleased me that I withdrew wholly from politics, with clean hands, I think, and enlisted in the Air Force . . .'

Nutting, Anthony
'Lawrence of Arabia: The Man and the Motive', 1961

LAWRENCE | OF | ARABIA | *The Man and the Motive* | by | ANTHONY NUTTING | LONDON | HOLLIS & CARTER | 1961

pp (1)–256 + map, illus, 22cm.

p (1), Half-title; verso, blank; frontispiece; p (3), Title-page; verso, Copyright etc; pp (5)–6, List of Contents; p (7), List of illustrations; p (8), Acknowledgements; pp (9)–16, Prologue; pp (17)–247, Text; pp (248)–9, Bibliography; p (250), blank; pp (251)–6, Index; + map.

This account of Lawrence's life accepts a great deal of what Lawrence himself wrote, though it does take into account the doubts that have been raised by other writers. Nutting concludes that the only satisfactory explanation of Lawrence's behaviour, especially after his return to England, is that he was a physical and mental masochist. In considering the two main problems discussed by Lawrence's other biographers, Nutting feels that he was not a homosexual and that this is substantiated by the majority of his friends and by a letter, seen by David Garnett, in which he wrote that he regarded the idea of a homosexual relationship as repellent.

In reviewing the question of the identity of S.A., Nutting considers the various theories put forward and concludes that 'in fact it is far more likely that S.A. was an imaginary conception, unrelated to a particular person or place, which represented all that he had found that was fair and gentle and lovable in Arabia and its peoples'. Nutting considers this to be a further enigma in Lawrence's life which leads him to the 'firm conviction that the key to the enigma is to be found in a combination of three things—masochism, fear of responsibility and mental breakdown'. In conclusion Nutting pays tribute to Lawrence's influence upon his friends and the gentle understanding that he could show. 'Perhaps no one put it quite so well as Gertrude Bell: "He lit so many fires in cold rooms".'

Ocampo, Victoria
'338171 T. E.', 1963

338171 T. E. | (LAWRENCE OF ARABIA) | by | VIC-TORIA OCAMPO | Translated by | DAVID GARNETT | LONDON | VICTOR GOLLANCZ LTD | 1963

pp (1)–128.

p (1), Half-title; verso, blank; p (3), Title; p (4), First published in French by Librairie Gallimard under the title | 338171 *T. E.* (*Lawrence d'Arabie*) | Copyright by Librairie Gallimard, 1947 | English translation: Victor Gollancz Ltd, 1963 | First published July 1963 | Second impression August 1963 | MADE AND PRINTED IN GREAT BRITAIN BY | THE GARDEN CITY PRESS LIMITED | LETCHWORTH, HERTFORD-SHIRE; p (5), Dedication; p (6), blank; p (7), Translator's note; p (8), blank; p (9), Quotation; p (10), blank; p (11), Contents; p (12), blank; pp 13–15, Introduction by A. W. Lawrence; p (16), blank; pp (17)–128, Text.

This work attempts an insight into Lawrence on the basis of his writings but without any personal knowledge of the man himself. It is a work in praise of Lawrence and elicited a glowing introduction from A. W. Lawrence who found it 'the most profound and the best-balanced of all portraits of my brother...

In fact, she loved him. That inexplicable phenomenon explains the uncanny truthfulness of her interpretation.'

Oxford High School for Boys
Proceedings at the Unveiling of the Memorial to Lawrence of Arabia, 3 October 1936
Oxford: 1937

Includes a speech by Sir Winston Churchill

Payne, Robert
'Lawrence of Arabia: A Triumph', 1966

ROBERT PAYNE | LAWRENCE OF ARABIA | A Triumph | *Illustrated and with map* | (device) | ROBERT HALE, LONDON

xiv + pp 15–256.

p (i), Half-title; verso, books by the same author; p (iii), Title-page; p (iv), Copyright, 1962, by Almat Publishing Corp | First published in Great Britain in a | revised edition in 1966 etc; p (v), Dedication; verso, blank; p (vii), Contents; p (viii), Map; p (ix), Illustrations; verso, blank; pp (xi)–xiii, Introduction; p (xiv), blank; pp 15–250, Text; pp (251)–6, Index

This is a readable account of Lawrence's life which draws heavily upon Lawrence's own writings. It presents a favourable account of Lawrence, and Payne describes him as one of the 'Terrible Avengers who demand from men the utmost in the service of perfect freedom'.

Pearman, Captain D. G.
'The Imperial Camel Corps with Colonel Lawrence', 1928
'The Imperial Camel Corps with Colonel Lawrence',
illustrated by a series of 89 lantern slides
and
'Lawrence and the Arab Revolt', illustrated by a series of
70 lantern slides
Lecture notes by Captain D. G. Pearman
Newton & Co Ltd, 43 Museum Street, WCI, 1928

p 1, Title and publisher's details, p 2, Acknowledgements; pp
3-4, Copy of a letter from Lawrence to Pearman; pp 5-21, Imperial Camel Corps notes on slides 1-89; pp 21-42, Lawrence
and the Arab Revolt notes on slides 1-70; pp 43-4, List of slides
numerically, not alphabetically, indexed.

Rattigan, Terence
'Ross', 1960

ROSS | *A Dramatic Portrait* | BY | TERENCE RATTIGAN
| (Device) | HAMISH HAMILTON | LONDON

pp (1)-122 + 1L, 19cm.

p (1), Half-title; verso, By the same author etc; p (3), Title-page;
verso, First published etc; p (5), Dedication; verso, blank; p (7),
Characters; verso, Cast of first production; pp 9-122, Text;
1L, blank.

The play begins with Lawrence's period in the RAF in 1922
and ends in the same period. Between these two acts, the scene
of the play shifts to the Middle East and deals in part with the
incident at Deraa. Although Rattigan based part of his play on

fact, a certain amount of fiction was introduced into the script. Lawrence's life is examined in relation to the incident at Deraa and the resultant effects on his mental state and his homosexual tendencies.

Richards, Vyvyan
'Portrait of T. E. Lawrence', 1936, English Edition

PORTRAIT OF | T. E. LAWRENCE | *THE LAWRENCE OF* | *THE SEVEN PILLARS OF WISDOM* | BY | VYVYAN RICHARDS | (Device)

pp 255

p (1), Half-title; verso, blank; frontispiece; p (3), Title; p (4), First published etc; p 5, Contents; p (6), blank; p 7, List of illustrations and maps; p (8), blank; pp 9–13, Introduction; p (14), blank; p 15, Acknowledgements; p (17), Half-title; p (18), blank; pp 19–252, Text; pp 253–5, Index; p (256), blank.

This work was issued immediately after Lawrence's death and presents an uncritical account of his life and achievements.

Robinson, Edward
'Lawrence the Rebel', 1946

LAWRENCE | THE | REBEL | BY | EDWARD ROBIN-SON | (Device) | LINCOLNS-PRAGER (PUBLISHERS) LTD | LONDON

1L + pp (1)–228 + 1L.

L 1, blank; frontispiece; p (1), Title; verso, First Edition Spring,

1946 etc; p 3, Introduction; p 4, Dedication; pp 5–225, Text; p 226, Acknowledgements; pp 227–8, Index.

The author was with Lawrence in the Arabian campaign and became 'an active participant in most of the campaign and "keeper of the records" '. It is intended to be a biography for the 'man in the street', and, therefore, gives a factual account of the situation as it happened, with footnote references to later developments. It is particularly interesting for the quotations given from notes that the author made during his period with Lawrence.

Rodman, Selden
'Lawrence, the Last Crusade: A dramatic narrative poem'
New York: Printed by the Haddon Craftsman, 1937

1L + pp 1–138 + 2Ls.

Rolls, S. C.
'Steel Chariots in the Desert', 1937 (re-issued 1940)

THE ODYSSEY LIBRARY | STEEL CHARIOTS | IN THE DESERT | by S. C. ROLLS | The Story of an Armoured-Car Driver with | the Duke of Westminster in Libya and in | Arabia with T. E. Lawrence | (Device) | JONATHAN CAPE | THIRTY BEDFORD SQUARE | LONDON

1L + pp (3)–(286) + 1L, 20cm.

1L, blank; p (3), Half-title; verso, Quotation from *Seven Pillars of Wisdom* (pp 591–2) regarding Rolls; p (5), Title-page; verso, First published May 1937 etc; pp 7–8, List of Contents; p 9, List of Illustrations and maps; p (10), blank; pp 11–12,

Extract from text regarding Rolls' first encounter with Lawrence; p 13, Preface; verso, blank; p 15, Half-title; verso, blank; pp 17–286, Text; + 1L, blank.

An extremely readable account of the Arab Revolt by one of the armoured car drivers attached to Feisal's army and subsequently Lawrence's driver. Although not a detailed study of events, it is of interest for the relationship of respect and admiration that existed between Rolls and Lawrence.

Rothenstein, William
'Twenty-Four Portraits by William Rothenstein, with Critical Appreciations by Various Hands'
London: George Allen & Unwin Ltd, 1920

(108)pp, illus, 25½cm.

A limited edition of 2,000 copies of which 1,200 were for sale in Great Britain and 800 in the USA.

References to Lawrence; pp 82–3.
A collection of portraits by the author with critical appreciations of the subjects by various writers. No name is ascribed to each portrait, but as David Hogarth is listed as a contributor it is possible that he was responsible for the appreciation on Lawrence.

Sherwood, Jane
'Post-Mortem Journal', 1964

Post-Mortem | Journal | *Communications from T. E. Lawrence* | JANE SHERWOOD | NEVILLE SPEARMAN | London 1964

1L + pp (1)–128 + 1L, 19cm.

L1, blank; p (1), Half-title; verso, blank; frontispiece; p (3), Title-page; verso, Publication details etc; p (5), Half-title; verso, blank; p (7), Contents; verso, blank; pp 9–13, Introduction; p (14), blank; pp 15–128, Text; L2, blank.

This is an account of spirit communications between Lawrence, under the name of Scott, through the mediumship of Jane Sherwood. The journal opens at the moment of Lawrence's death and continues until 1959, the first communication being in 1938. It shows the mental torture which Lawrence faced after his death due to the weaknesses and vanities of his earthly life. As to the credibility of this work, one can only quote from Mrs Sherwood's statement on the dust jacket: 'As to the validity of the information contained in Scott's journal I can only vouch for my own honesty; . . . The reader must judge of its probability for himself.'

Smith, Clare Sydney
'The Golden Reign', 1940 (Pocket Edition 1949)

THE GOLDEN REIGN | *The story of my friendship with* | 'LAWRENCE OF ARABIA' | CLARE SYDNEY | SMITH

pp (1)–190 + 1L, illus, 17½cm.

p (1), Half-title; verso, Publication details; p (3), Title-page; verso, Printed in Great Britain etc; p (5), Foreword by Mrs S. Lawrence; verso, blank; pp (7)–185, Text; p (186), blank; pp (187)–190, Index; + 1L, blank.

This biography of Lawrence is by the wife of his commanding officer at Mount Batten RAF station. It presents an interesting account of Lawrence's life in the RAF until his death in 1935.

Sperber, Manes
'The Achilles Heel', by Manes Sperber, translated by
Constantine FitzGibbon
London: Andre Deutsch, 1959

224pp, index, 22cm.

The essay on Lawrence entitled 'False Situations: T. E. Lawrence and his Two Legends' appears on pp 173–204.

Sperber examines Aldington's work on Lawrence and concludes that he failed to destroy the legend. He then proceeds to examine two legends of Lawrence: (1) as a Napoleonic figure, which he maintains is open to question and could have been weakened had Aldington concentrated his attack upon it; and (2) 'the legend of repentance', which could only have been destroyed if *Seven Pillars* had been as bad a book as Aldington maintained and if Lawrence's career had not taken the form it did.

Storrs, Ronald
'Orientations', by Ronald Storrs
London: Nicholson & Watson, 1937

xviii, 557pp, illus, maps, index, 21cm.

This work is the autobiography of a Civil Servant who held several posts of importance in the Middle East. He was in the Ministry of Finance of the Egyptian government 1904–9, Assistant Political Officer with the EEF in 1917, Military Liaison Officer in Baghdad and Mesopotamia 1917–20, and afterwards Civil Governor of Jerusalem. He was also responsible for the initial intricate negotiations with Hussein and his son during the period before the outbreak of war until the declaration of the Revolt in 1916.

As such, he knew Lawrence intimately both in a private and official capacity, and had a great respect for him and his part in the Arab Revolt. The references to Lawrence are too numerous to detail separately as they form a thread throughout the book, which is also of importance for its description of events in the Middle East through the eyes of a gifted administrator.

Thomas, Lowell
'With Lawrence in Arabia', 1925

WITH | LAWRENCE | IN ARABIA | (rule) | by | LOWELL THOMAS | (rule) | WITH FRONTISPIECE AND 30 OTHER | ILLUSTRATIONS | HUTCHINSON & CO | (*Publishers*) *Ltd* | LONDON | (rule)

pp (1)–(255), 21cm.

p (1), Half-title; verso, blank; frontispiece; p (3), Title-page; verso, Publication details; p (5), Dedication; verso, Publisher's note; pp (7)–(8), List of Contents; pp (9)–(10), List of Illustrations; pp 11-14, Introduction by Lowell Thomas; plate; pp 15–254, Text; p (255), Reprint of tribute by Field Marshal Viscount Allenby broadcast of 19 May 1935 and printed in *The Listener*; + 1 blank page.

The work of Thomas was published as a result of his very successful lecture tours on Lawrence and bears the mark of a newspaperman whose purpose was to publicise the war for the morale of the civilian population in America. Consequently, his book is a highly readable but uncritical account of Lawrence's activities in Arabia.

A copy of this work, which Lawrence had given to a friend, T. E. Willis, was offered for sale at Sotheby in December 1971. It contained annotations by Lawrence, some of which were initialled. All of the comments point to inaccuracies in the text and the longest initialled note gives the reason why Thomas's account of his first meeting with Lawrence is untrue.

Toynbee, Arnold J.
'Acquaintances', by Arnold J. Toynbee
London: OUP, 1967

(viii), 312pp, illus, index, 22cm.

The essay on Lawrence falls on pp 178–97 and deals mainly with his encounters with Lawrence at the Paris Conference and specifically with the problem of Lawrence's relations with the Arabs and the Sykes-Picot agreement. He considers that Lawrence could be considered a great man if one accepts that greatness in a human being is the capacity to move other human beings. Regarding Lawrence's actions after the war, Toynbee accepts the oft quoted reason of disappointment about the Arab cause.

Villars, Jean Beraud
'T. E. Lawrence: or the Search for the Absolute', 1958

T. E. LAWRENCE | OR | THE SEARCH FOR THE ABSOLUTE | *By* | JEAN BERAUD VILLARS | TRANSLATED FROM THE FRENCH BY | PETER DAWNAY | SIDGWICK AND JACKSON LIMITED | LONDON

pp (i)–xii + pp (1)–358, frontis, maps, 22cm.

p (i), blank; verso, blank; frontispiece; p (iii), Title-page; verso, Printing details; p (v), Dedication; verso, blank; p (vii), Publisher's note; p (viii), blank; pp (ix)–x, List of Contents; pp (xi)–

xii, Preface; pp (1)–353; Text; p (354), blank; pp (355)–358, bibliography.

This book on Lawrence was first published in French in 1955 and so fails to take into account Aldington's biography, which appeared in the same year. Villars' work is certainly sympathetic though he does come to the conclusion that in his private life Lawrence was homosexual. It uses a great deal of Bremond's book, *Le Hedjaz dans la guerre mondiale*, which was published in 1931, and represents the French viewpoint of the Middle East during World War I. Villars feels that Bremond's book is full of rancour and inaccurate in places, and that often 'he is led away by passion'.

Weintraub, Stanley
'Private Shaw and Public Shaw', 1963

PRIVATE SHAW | *and* | PUBLIC SHAW | (rule) | *a dual portrait of* | *Lawrence of Arabia and G.B.S.* | (rule) | *by* STANLEY WEINTRAUB | (device) | JONATHAN CAPE, *Thirty Bedford Square, London*

xvi, + pp (1)–302.

p (i), Half-title; verso, Facsimile of G. B. Shaw's inscription in Lawrence's copy of Saint Joan and the note by Lawrence which appears on the verso; p (iii), Title-page; verso, First published in Great Britain 1963 etc; p (v), Dedication; verso, blank; p (vii), Quotation; verso, blank; p (ix), List of Contents; p (x), blank; p (xi), List of Illustrations; verso, blank; pp xiii–xvi, Foreword; 1L, Half-title; verso, blank; frontispiece; pp 1–281, Text; p 282, blank; pp 283–7, Appendix; pp 288–94, References; pp 295–6, bibliography; pp 297–302, Index.

This work covers only the twelve years beginning in 1922

which formed the duration of the friendship between Lawrence and George Bernard Shaw, ending with Lawrence's death in 1935. It only touches on the Lawrence of Arabia legend where it is pertinent to the association between the two men. The book also deals with the relationship between Lawrence and Shaw's *Saint Joan* which is commented upon in the periodical article section (see p 165).

Shaw also advised Lawrence on the manuscript of *The Seven Pillars* and he recommended that Lawrence should cut the first chapter as it was a bad beginning. Villars considers that Shaw realised 'that these preliminary statements would remove all credence from the work'. Shaw always denied that his suggested excisions were because of the political implications and indeed, when the suppressed chapter was published in *Oriental Assembly*, Shaw again stressed that the omitted chapter was a bad opening and that politics did not enter into it. 'I advised various cuts in the same way one cuts the first draft of a play. There were many libellous passages, and Lawrence was delighted when I suggested I should rewrite them and allow him to say all he wanted to say in perfectly legal phraseology.'

This is an extremely readable work which deals in great detail with Lawrence's friendship with the Shaws and throws light on the later years of his life.

Williamson, Henry
'Genius of Friendship', 1941

GENIUS OF FRIENDSHIP | '*T. E. LAWRENCE*' | (rule) | HENRY WILLIAMSON | FABER AND FABER LIMITED | 24 Russell Square | LONDON

p (1)–78 + 1L.

pp (1)–4, blank; p (5), Half-title; p (6), blank; p (7), Title; p (8),
First published in November Mcmxli | by Faber and Faber Limited |
24 Russell Square, London, WC1 | Printed in Great Britain by |
R. MacLehose and Company Limited | The University Press
Glasgow | All rights reserved | ; pp 9–78, Text; 1L, blank.

This work deals with the friendship between Lawrence and
Williamson, which began in 1928 after Lawrence had written to
Williamson, through Edward Garnett, regarding his reactions
to *Tarka the Otter*. This friendship was cultivated by Williamson
when he found 'That the friendship or companionship I had
always been seeking in life, so far in vain, was possible'. On 13
May 1935 Williamson sent a letter to Lawrence regarding the
menace of Nazism, writing: 'You alone are capable of negotiat-
ing with Hitler . . . I must speak to you about this immediately'.
It was whilst sending a telegram to Williamson, arranging to
meet him at Clouds Hill, that Lawrence met with the fatal
accident avoiding two cyclists.

Wilson, Colin
'The Outsider', by Colin Wilson
London: Gollancz, 1956

288pp, notes, 21cm.

The essay on Lawrence is contained in Chapter Four (pp 70–84)
and he is considered together with Van Gogh and Nijinsky. The
problem as seen by Wilson is one of the 'Outsider' attempting
to gain control of his own destiny and a seeking for identity. In
considering the latter, Wilson quotes from Kennington's contribution to *T. E. Lawrence by his Friends* in which he wrote of a
schoolmaster's reaction to *The Seven Pillars* which was: 'He has
found an "I" but it is not a true "I" . . . He is never alive in what

he does.' This conclusion is also reached by Malraux in his essay 'Lawrence and the demon of the absolute' (see p 149).

Wilson also considers Lawrence's interest in ascetic religious discipline and his pre-occupation with pain which 'was an invaluable instrument in experiments to determine the extent of his moral freedom'. He considers that it is the spiritual aspect of Lawrence's life which has not been treated adequately by any of his biographers, and that Aldington's Freudian analysis was wholly inadequate especially as the question was answered by *Seven Pillars* which said 'Man is not a unity; he is many. But for anything to be worth doing, he must become a unity.' This, Wilson maintains, introduces a further consideration of the Outsider: that of the prophetic element.

Section D

Articles about T. E. Lawrence

Aldington, Richard
 Richard Aldington defends his book
Daily Mail (London), 1 February 1955

Aldington, Richard
 Why I debunked the Lawrence legend
Illustrated, 2 February 1955

Allenby, Viscount
 Tribute to Lawrence of Arabia in war
The Listener (London), 22 May 1935, pp 857–8
A reprint of a broadcast made on 19 May, the day of Lawrence's
death. It is a brief tribute from Lawrence's commander in which
he pays tribute to the Middle East campaign and his brilliant
leadership.

Alvarez, A.
 Ross, by T. Rattigan (criticism)
New Statesman (London), 21 May 1960, p 750

Anderson, Patrick
 The Desert Prince
The Spectator (London), 25 December 1964, p 875
A review of *The Letters of T. E. Lawrence*, edited by David
Garnett, which attempts to relate the letters to Lawrence's public
image, and concludes that 'whatever was warmly virtuous in
Lawrence the man rarely got through his self consciousness on
to the paper'.

Arendt, Hannah
 The Imperialistic Character
The Review of Politics, Vol 12, No 3, July 1950, pp 303–20
The article discusses the character and quality of the administra-
tors of the British Empire in India, Egypt and South Africa.
'The author of the imperialistic legend is Rudyard Kipling, its

topic is the British Empire, its result the Imperialistic character (after all the only true character form of modern times). And while the legend of the British Empire has little to do with the realities of British imperialism, it forced or deluded into its services the best sons of England.'

After a general consideration of this theme, using Lord Cromer of Egypt as an example, the discussion then moves on to the British Secret Service which can also lay claim to a legend 'the legend of the Great Game as told by Rudyard Kipling in Kim'. In considering this aspect of the imperialist character, Lawrence is used as an example of the adventurer turned secret agent whose motives were destroyed by the politicians. Lawrence felt that he belonged to the 'lost generation' because 'the old men came out again and took from us our victory' in order to 're-make [the world] in the likeness of the former world they knew', although this sentiment was dropped from later editions of *The Seven Pillars of Wisdom* on the advice of George Bernard Shaw. The author feels that Lawrence had to behave as if the Arab national movement was his prime interest and he took the part so well that he came to believe in it himself and 'he took great delight in a role that demanded a reconditioning of his whole personality until he fitted into the Great Game, until he became the incarnation of the force of the Arab national movement'.

The article attempts to analyse the motives and actions following the Arab Revolt and concludes that his actions were the seeking of another role motivated by the realisation that 'he himself had not been big, but only the role which he had aptly assumed, that his bigness had been the result of the Game and not a product by himself'.

Armitage, Flora
The Home of Lawrence of Arabia

Contemporary Review, January 1953, pp 35–9
A detailed description of Lawrence's cottage at Clouds Hill, together with a description of the Kennington effigy of Lawrence in St Martin's Church, Wareham.

Baker, Sir Herbert
Tribute to Lawrence of Arabia—In peace
The Listener (London), 22 May 1935, p 858
A reprint of a broadcast made on 19 May which praises Lawrence's knowledge of medieval architecture, his insight into the war and his appreciation of the arts.

Barker, A. R. V.
  Revolt in the Desert (review)
World Today (New York), April 1927, pp 445–50, illus

Barnett, R. D.
  T. E. Lawrence and the British Museum (letter)
Times Literary Supplement (London), 16 October 1969

Bates, H. E.
  The Mint is bound to shock (review)
News Chronicle (London), 14 February 1955

Boak, D.
  Malraux and T. E. Lawrence
Modern Language Review, April 1966, pp 218–24

Bolt, Robert
  Clues to the legend of Lawrence
New York Times Magazine, 25 February 1962, pp 16–17, 45, 48, 50, illus
A personal evaluation of Lawrence's life, achievements and personality by the scriptwriter for the film *Lawrence of Arabia*. He begins by accepting the premise that Lawrence was a homo-

sexual by nature if not by practice but that this was irrelevant to his role in the Arab Revolt.

Bolt examines *Seven Pillars*, upon which he based his screen-play, and concludes that lies are evident in this book but not lies for the purpose of self-aggrandizement, as many of them were detrimental. In the book Bolt discerns the dual personality evident in the writing of the book with the 'I' in the book some-times taking on the characteristics of a third party. The book should be viewed from the classical idealism of the period which showed itself in the patriotic attitude towards the world war.

The article ends by considering the post-war Lawrence and Bolt concludes that he was a man of divided loyalties who, despite knowing that Britain's promises to the Arabs would not be kept, did try to salvage some of the Arab cause at the peace conference. In considering his attempt to be Ross and to be Shaw, Bolt concludes that he failed because 'he had committed himself too deeply and had to remain a figure from an epic— Lawrence of Arabia. I think that is why there are so many lies and so much misplaced poetry in the book [*Seven Pillars*]. It is a poem about a poem already written. For two years he had lived a literary mode, impermissibly.'

Although this article has nothing new to say about Lawrence, its interest lies in the light that it throws on Bolt's interpretation of Lawrence which formed the basis for the film which once again brought Lawrence before the public.

Brien, A.
Ross, by T. Rattigan (criticism)
The Spectator (London), 20 May 1960, p 732

Brooke, J.
Men and books—The Downward Urge
Time and Tide, 19 February 1955
Review of *The Mint*.

Butler, P. R.

T. E. Lawrence

Quarterly Review, Vol CCLXVI, April 1936, pp 219–34

A review of the trade edition of *Seven Pillars of Wisdom* which, although uncritical of the book, proves to be a reasoned examination of the work. The reviewer has taken topics for consideration, beginning with Lawrence's descriptions of the Arabs and Arabia which he feels touch 'chords deep down in one's heart' and although others have described Arabia, 'to Lawrence has it been reserved to glory in Arabian scenery and to pass its glory to us'.

Also considered in depth by the reviewer is the suffering which Lawrence underwent, beginning with the killing of Hamed and Farraj, the first an act of retribution and the second an act of mercy to prevent his wounded friend from falling into the hands of the Turks. This aspect is further illustrated by the incident that took place in the hospital at Damascus when Lawrence, after prodigious efforts to get the hospital working, was assailed by a medical major regarding the state of the hospital and 'At this onslaught I cackled out like a chicken with the wild laughter of strain'. The point is also made that Lawrence was not without humour and that this is reflected as much by the illustrations to the book as by the text.

Candler, E.

Lawrence of the Hedjaz

Atlantic Monthly, March 1926, pp 289–304

Carrington, C. E.

Men and books

Time and Tide, 5 February 1955

Review of *Lawrence of Arabia: A biographical enquiry*, by Aldington.

Charles, M.
Revolt in the Desert (review)
New Republic, 25 May 1927, pp 24–5

Champress, H. M.
Prince of Mecca
The Spectator (London), 4 February 1955
Review of Aldington's book.

Churchill, A.
The Soldier of mystery
Time and Tide, 11/17 July 1963, p 25
A review of *338171 T. E. (Lawrence of Arabia)*, by Victoria
Ocampo.

Coates, J. G.
(Reply to article by Gendzier in Spring 1965 issue)
Middle East Journal, Autumn 1965, pp 556–7

Coleman, J.
El Aurens
New Statesman, 14 December 1962, p 877

———

Colonel Lawrence—A denial
Morning Post, 28 December 1929
A news item about Lawrence's activities in India.

———

Colonel Lawrence's manuscript
Journal of the Central Asia Society, Vol XIII, Part II, pp 165–8
A review of the manuscript of *Seven Pillars* which was housed
in the Bodleian Library to be read but not quoted from or published. The review is extremely favourable but it is hampered
by the restriction on quotations and the fact that the work was,

at that time, unpublished and had not been subjected to any searching examination.

___

Colonel T. E. Lawrence
Morning Post, 27 September 1928
An amusing news item about Lawrence's supposed activities in the Punjab disguised as a saint.

Corbett, H. A.
A critic in action
Royal United Services Institute Journal, November 1963, pp 358–65

___

Correspondence on the extent of Lawrence's Arabic
The Times Literary Supplement, 8, 15, 22, 29 June & 13, 20 July 1951

___

Counterfeit or true
The Times Literary Supplement, 18 February 1955
An article on Lawrence built around a review of Aldington's biographical enquiry.

Cross, L. B.
Lawrence of Arabia (an appreciation)
Modern Churchman, July 1935, pp 236–42
This is the text of a sermon preached in the Chapel of Jesus College, Oxford, on 26 May 1935, by Rev L. B. Cross, MA, Fellow of Jesus College, Vice-Principal of Ripon Hall. In the sermon parallels are drawn between Lawrence and Christ although stressing that no suggestion is made that he was as great as Christ, merely that similarities do exist. The first comparisons drawn are the similarities between the period of preparation for their life's work which in each case covered

three years. Secondly, each man experienced similar treatment from society and in each case an ascetic quality existed as did the need for each man to humble himself in the eyes of others.

The article should of course be considered in the light of the circumstances under which the sermon was delivered, namely a memorial service at Lawrence's former college.

Davies, H. Hier
Lawrence and Feisal: their encounter at Suez (letter)
Morning Post, 13 September 1933

Dawse, Y. A.
Lawrence at Clouds Hill
Chambers Journal, March 1940, pp 207–8
A brief description of Lawrence's cottage at Clouds Hill though not as detailed as the one by Flora Armitage (see p 128).

Dayton, J.
Tracking the train Lawrence wrecked
The Times (London), 4 September 1964, p 13, map
A visit to the present-day remains of Lawrence's demolition work on the Hedjaz railway.

———

Death of a Hero
Private Eye (London), September 1969
Deals with the publication history of Aldington's work.

Dent, A.
Lawrence of Arabia (review of film)
Illustrated London News, 18 January 1963, p 100

Devers, C. M.
With Lawrence of Arabia in the Ranks: Personal recollections of a Private in the Tank Corps
The World Today, July 1927, pp 141–4

This article was prompted by the publication of *The Seven Pillars of Wisdom* and is the observations of a private who served, 'at the time unknowingly', with Lawrence in the Tank Corps. It presents a portrait of Lawrence as a soldier somewhat divorced from his fellow men, as 'Shaw seemed unapproachable and unapproachable in the sense that he seemed to inspire respect, mere private soldier that he was. He was, if I may put it, above and apart . . .' The author conveys an impression of the type of life Lawrence lived in the Tank Corps without really telling the reader a great deal about the man.

Dixon, D.
Very superior
Motor Cycle, 3 October 1963
Describes T. E. Lawrence's Brough Superior, GW 2275.

Donoghue, D.
Ross, by T. Rattigan (criticism)
Hudson Review, Spring 1961, pp 97–9

Doyle, Katie
Lawrence of Arabia and Mount Batten
The Independent (Plymouth), 29 January 1967, pp 14–15, illus
An account of Lawrence's life in the Royal Air Force at Mount Batten, especially his connections with the development of high speed rescue launches and his friendship with Clare Sydney Smith (see p 117).

Duncan, T.
Lawrence—thirty years after
Viewpoints, Vol V, No 5, 1965

Engle, Anita
The Mysterious S.A.
The New Statesman and Nation, 22 December 1956, pp 812–13

A biographical sketch of Sarah Aaronsohn, leader of a spy ring in Palestine, which provided Allenby with information about the Turkish army which proved of great value to the Allies, and indeed Allenby credited the organisation with saving the lives of at least 30,000 British soldiers.

It was felt by some people that she was in fact the S.A. to whom Lawrence dedicated *Seven Pillars of Wisdom* and this idea was raised by Graves in response to Aldington's contention that S.A. was really an Arab boy nicknamed Sheikh Achmed. The author maintains that even if Lawrence had dedicated the book to Aaronsohn, which was unlikely, there was no foundation in any of the stories 'of the romance, which pops up in the English press from time to time, always with more exotic embellishments. I was able to establish this fact conclusively only three months ago, from members of the family who still live in Zichron Yascow.' The article then continues to discuss the 'Nili' movement, the part played in it by Sarah Aaronsohn, and the effect that it had on the Allied war effort.

Findlay, C.
The Amazing A.C.2.
The Listener, 5 June 1958, pp 937–8, illus
An account of Lawrence's early days in the RAF (1922) by his Adjutant.

Fitzgibbon, Constance
The Lawrence legend
Encounter, 1960, pp 55–6

Forster, E. M.
Clouds Hill
The Listener, 1 September 1938, pp 426–7, illus

Forster, E. M.
  The Mint
The Listener, 17 February 1955, pp 279–80
A balanced review by Forster, who was in communication with
Lawrence during the writing of *The Mint.*

Forster, E. M.
  Seven Pillars of Wisdom (review)
The Listener, 31 July 1935, p 211

Garnett, David
  Lawrence in the dock
New Statesman, 5 February 1955, pp 182–4
A review of *The Mint*

Garnett, David
  Letters (of T. E. Lawrence)
Atlantic Monthly, February/March 1939, pp 147–57, 327–37

Gaster, Z.
  Lawrence and King Hussein, the 1921 negotiations
National Review, 15 October 1938, p 512
This paper discusses the relations between Lawrence and King
Hussein after the Near East Conference in 1921 which was the
first meeting between the two men. This account of the
negotiations between them is based on the reminiscences of El
Khatib Bey who was at that time the Hedjaz Minister in Cairo
intimately involved in the negotiations. The paper discusses the
mistrust that developed between the two men as Hussein felt
that the British had broken the promises made at the time of the
Arab Revolt. Khatib Bey was of the opinion, however, that
Lawrence's offer was the best that could be expected in the light
of the political realities of the situation.

Gendzier, Irene
  Notes on T. E. Lawrence
  Middle East Journal, Spring 1965, pp 259–61
  The article discusses the supposed mystery surrounding Lawrence and concludes that he did supply several of the answers in various letters and comments. The decision to join the ranks of the Air Force was motivated by a sense of failure at the Arab Revolt and a desire to 'frequent a spiritual underworld which rapidly gained mastery over him'.

Gill, F. C.
  T. E. Lawrence, his life
  Methodist Magazine, July 1949, pp 322–6

Graves, Robert
  Lawrence of Arabia—a reply to A. T. Wilson
  The Sunday Times (London), 31 July 1927

Graves, Robert
  The Lawrence I knew
  News Chronicle (London), 31 January 1955

Graves, Robert
  The Riddle of S.A. of the Seven Pillars of Wisdom (letter)
  The Sunday Times (London), 23 June 1968

Graves, Robert
  T. E. Lawrence and the riddle of S.A.
  Saturday Review, 15 June 1963, pp 16–17
  Followed by correspondence in issue of 6 July 1963.

Greig, T. P.
  Seven Pillars of Wisdom: a bibliographical note
  Morning Post, 14 November 1928

The article begins with a brief examination of T. German-Reed's *Bibliographical Notes on T. E. Lawrence's Seven Pillars of Wisdom and Revolt in the Desert*, which is criticised because of its incompleteness. The most important omission is of any reference to the Oxford text of *The Seven Pillars of Wisdom*, especially in view of the fact that Lawrence had issued his own bibliographical notes to subscribers in 1927. The article then continues with notes on the Oxford Text and the limited edition of *The Seven Pillars of Wisdom*.

Grigson, G.
Colonel Lawrence and his unorthodox views of Homer
Morning Post, 16 August 1935

Grindle, H.
The Seven Pillars of Wisdom (review)
Central Literary Magazine, January 1939, pp 23-30

Guthrie, J.
Call me Ishmael
Literary Guide, 30 January 1955
A review of Aldington's book.

Hart, B. H. Liddell
A genius of war and letters; the desert revolt
The Times (London), 20 May 1935, pp 15-16, illus

Hart, B. H. Liddell
T. E. Lawrence: Aldington and the truth
London Magazine, April 1955, pp 67-75
A defence of Lawrence against the theories put forward in Aldington's biography of Lawrence '. . . his book reads like the report of a backstairs inquiry by a private detective looking through keyholes'.

Hart, B. H. Liddell

T. E. Lawrence: through his own eyes and another's
Southern Review, Vol 2, No 1, 1936, pp 22–40
The publication of *The Seven Pillars of Wisdom* in America led
to this article which, although it is an examination of the book,
is really a reappraisal of Lawrence. He begins by welcoming the
publication as a 'necessary service for the purification of legend'
because 'there is no more mistaken service than the withholding
of a man's own evidence from the feeling that haste is indecent
and in the belief that the passage of time will produce a clearer
atmosphere. Early publication is a more hopeful step towards
purification'. *The Seven Pillars* is considered to be an improve-
ment on *Revolt in the Desert* mainly because it contains much of
Lawrence's thought that was edited from the abridgement.
Even so the complete book cannot be considered '. . . a complete revelation even at the time when it was written. It was
too conscious a pursuit of artistic achievement.'

This appraisal should be read bearing in mind its date and the
fact that little new information had appeared on Lawrence. In
the circumstances it is not surprising that Liddell Hart accepts
many of Lawrence's statements, especially with regard to his
relations with the Arabs, the desert and his idealistic motives.
The second part of the article is concerned with the military side
of the Revolt and Liddell Hart places it into the campaign as a
whole and considers it to have been of great value in protecting
Allenby's flank and in occupying Turkish troops. He also considers Lawrence's guerrilla tactics to be ideally suited to the
occasion as 'in view of the fact that the Turks had scantier
reserves of material than of men, "killing engines" was a more
deadly strategy than "killing Turks" '. In considering Lawrence
as a commander, he praises Lawrence very highly and one can
only speculate as to how much of this was influenced by Lawrence's 'Evolution of a Revolt'.

The article concludes by looking at Lawrence's period in the Air Force and yet again the suggestion of a monastic parallel is used as Liddell Hart writes: 'It may be near the truth to say that he enlisted in the Air Force for the same reason that thoughtful men in the Middle Ages entered a monastery.' In conclusion he considers that Lawrence had a fundamental goodness with faults that were near the surface and virtues that were profound. 'In contrast to one's experience with others, the deeper one penetrated the more difficult it became to gauge his limits, until one was forced to admit that here was a man bigger in personality and intellect than any other one had known. His greatness can be judged to some extent by his works, if examined, and the impression he made on others, in close contact.'

Hartley, L. P.
A failed masterpiece
The Listener, 14 April 1955, pp 658–9
Concludes that *The Mint* is admirable in many ways but it is too tightly written and too condensed.

Haverstick, J.
Behind the book (review of *The Mint*)
Saturday Review, 2 April 1955, p 21

———

Hero as rookie (review of *The Mint*)
Time (New York), 21 March 1955, p 108

Hill, M.
T. E. Lawrence: some trivial memories
Virginia Quarterly Review, October 1945, pp 587–96
An interesting account of a friendship with Lawrence, mainly because the author is a woman and very few women could really say that they had a friendship with Lawrence. In fact the author prefers to call it a comradeship 'since so many have claimed the

friendship that was never lightly given'. Again one finds that people who knew him were distrustful of his public image. 'The Lawrence cult, the Lawrence legend, the order and eloquence of words spoken, arouse in me a wonder whether the Lawrence I once knew . . . had ever lived at all.'

The author first met Lawrence when he was working with Woolley for the British Museum in 1921. A mutual interest was found in an admiration for James Elroy Flecker which was re-kindled when the author and her husband were transferred to the consulate at Jaffa. The reminiscences in this article are mainly of a trivial nature but they do provide insights into the Lawrence behind the headlines, although the author admits that it is difficult to describe him as 'He was faceted to a thousand different angles, and the particular facet one caught and called Lawrence depended on the angle at which one caught it. That, I think, is why no satisfactorily homogeneous individual emerges, as sculptors say, "in the round", either from his own writings or the many concerning him. One can only try to describe the Lawrence one knew, without pretension that it was any more a real Lawrence than the next man's.'

Again one is presented with the picture of a man who called on his friends at irregular intervals and without prior warning, but on each occasion after a few moments it seemed as if the last visit was only the day before. This quality of friendship is one that is rarely found but seems to have been the feeling of all Lawrence's real friends (cf Kennington's article on p 145).

Hogarth, D. G.
Lawrence of Arabia: story of his book
The Times, 13 December 1926
Review of *The Seven Pillars of Wisdom*.

Howe, Irving
T. E. Lawrence: the problem of heroism

Hudson Review, Autumn 1962, pp 333-64
This lengthy article begins by considering why Lawrence still seems to matter and concludes that it is because 'He is not yet a name to put away in history, a footnote in dust. He continues to arouse sympathy, outrage, excitement . . . The dynamiter of railways turned out to be an intellectual harassed by ambition and guilt.'

The early background of Lawrence's life is sketched in, including his illegitimacy and his interest in history and archaeology prior to his joining the British Museum dig at Carchemish. In discussing Lawrence's archaeological work the article stresses the fact that part of this work was a guise for mapping work for the army and Howe feels that in this case 'Aldington's claim was correct when he stated that "None of the intellectual writing on Lawrence had expressed the faintest regret or indignation at this official abuse of science and religion to screen politico-military tactics" '. This consideration has been further reinforced by Knightley and Simpson who lay stress on Lawrence's early intelligence activities and the real power which he possessed despite his apparent junior position according to his rank.

In considering Lawrence's part in the Arab Revolt, Howe considers that 'The picture of Lawrence plunging into the chaos of the Arab world, measuring the worth of its leaders and quickly bringing order to its ranks—this picture is surely overdrawn if one judges by the limited powers Lawrence actually enjoyed at the moment'. This judgement can perhaps be questioned now if one considers the evidence produced by Knightley and Simpson which seems to indicate that Lawrence's authority far exceeded his apparent position. In discussing the revolt, the problem of heroism is the main theme, beginning with the way in which Lawrence began to participate in the revolt, undertaking 'the Arab campaign as an adventure' but one which turned sour as 'His apparent fufilment of the hero's tasks was undercut at every point by a distrust and mockery of the idea of heroism'. This point was taken up by Read in his review of *The Seven Pillars of Wisdom* (see p 156) when he concluded that Lawrence did not match up to the epic hero, but this is considered by Howe to be the reason for the continuing interest in Lawrence as 'For better or worse, the hero as he appears in the tangle of modern life is a man struggling with a vision he can neither realise nor abandon'.

The third part of the article begins with the Paris Peace Conference and Lawrence's arguments in presenting the Arab case against all odds as it was inevitable that France was going to be given Syria. This, together with the writing of *Seven Pillars* proved to be a great strain on Lawrence but Howe considers the result to be a great book although as 'A biography "The Seven Pillars of Wisdom" is veiled, ambiguous, misleading, less a direct revelation than a performance from which the truth can be wrenched'. Howe feels that Lawrence's sense of purposelessness and a suffering from nihilism provides the clue to the real Lawrence and to his life in the Air Force. In conclusion he considers that Lawrence's letters give a more faithful picture of his life than the books written about him. 'Like much of his life, his death was no completion, it failed to round off his drama or his problem. He left his name entangled with a cluster of unanswered questions, this prince of our disorder.'

Johns, W. E.
How Lawrence joined the RAF
The Sunday Times (London), 8 April 1951
An account of Lawrence's attempt to join the Air Force and in particular the problems of obtaining medical clearance for him.

Kedourie, E.
Colonel Lawrence
Cambridge Journal, June 1954, pp 515–30

An examination of Lawrence and his motives which draws the following conclusion: 'What interested him rather were his own sensations, and to see how he could manipulate events'.

Kennington, E. H.
An unofficial portrait
Atlantic Monthly, April 1937, pp 406–15
This article is important for the two main threads which run through it, the first being the illustrations for *The Seven Pillars of Wisdom*, and the second the mental anguish of Lawrence. Kennington's first contact with Lawrence was through one of Lowell Thomas's lectures at the Albert Hall which was followed by Lawrence's purchase of two of Kennington's pictures. This led to a meeting at All Souls during which Lawrence raised the problem of the illustrations for *The Seven Pillars* which he wanted done from photographs. On being told that this would be an unsatisfactory method, Lawrence remarked 'What a pity! For my sitters are in various parts of Arabia' and it was then that Kennington offered to travel to Arabia to draw them.

The trip was made by Kennington whilst Lawrence was at a conference in Cairo and the drawings were made in Damascus, Jerusalem and Amman. It was on this trip that Lawrence appeared from Cairo for a brief visit and Kennington was moved by the reception that the Arabs gave to 'Aurens' although 'I thought he got warmth and pleasure from their love, but now know his pain also, for they longed for him to lead them again into Damascus, this time to drive out the French . . . He was apart but they did not know it. They loved him, and gave him all their hearts.' The illustrations were done and Lawrence selected eighteen of them offering Kennington £720 for them although he did not really want payment. The problem of the preparation of *The Seven Pillars of Wisdom* is discussed, especially the problem of persuading Lawrence that the book should be published. Indeed he felt obliged to show Kennington the book only because he had done the illustrations and not because Lawrence felt that the work had any merit.

It is at this stage that the article begins to be concerned with the torment going on in Lawrence's mind and during a visit to Clouds Hill with the printer, whilst Lawrence was in the Tank Corps, Kennington was surprised at his condition as 'He was possessed of devils, visibly thinner, pale, scared and savage. He seemed to avoid looking at me and when he did his look was hostile . . .' On a further visit to Kennington's house it was evident that Lawrence was undergoing a protracted torture as 'There was a wall of pain between him and us . . . That was the only time I saw T.E. on the edge of madness.' After the publication of the limited edition, the contact between them became less frequent and at times his visits were of pain to Kennington although 'so serene were his following visits that one had to forget the pain'. The contact between the two men is probably best expressed by Kennington's feelings about Lawrence. 'In the last year or two I saw him rarely; he was continually present spiritually, with help, understanding, joy and jokes. His physical presence—though it, like his letters, spelled happiness—seemed unnecessary.'

Kern, E.
Desert revolt urged on by a legendary Englishman
Life (New York), 20 October 1967, pp 54–5

Kirby, H. T.
Lawrence of Arabia—Brass rubber!
Apollo, July 1938, pp 18–19, illus
This article followed the publication of *T. E. Lawrence by his Friends* which revealed his interest in brass rubbing. Lawrence's rubbings were presented to the Ashmolean Museum and the manuscript catalogue of the collection was amended and cor-

rected in Lawrence's own handwriting. Two of the rubbings are reproduced and both are felt to be particularly fine examples.

Kirkbridge, A. C.
   T. E. Lawrence: a memory of the Hedjaz 1918
   Manchester Guardian, 20 August 1956, p 4

Lamplugh, Lois
   Happy years of T. E. Lawrence
Western Morning News (Plymouth), 22 January 1971, p 6
This covers the period that Lawrence spent at Mount Batten and in particular his campaign for reforms in the service routine, the high speed rescue launches and the Schneider trophy contest.

   Lawrence and his legend (review of Aldington's book)
The Times (London), 2 February 1955

   Lawrence of Arabia—startling attack on uncrowned king
The Sunday Times (London), 24 July 1927

   Lawrence of Arabia: venture in debunking
Newsweek (New York), 8 February 1954, p 88
A short article concerning the attempts by Aldington to find an American publisher for a book on Lawrence. Apparently negotiations were not too successful until news of the book was broken in the London *Evening Standard* which brought Lawrence right back into the public's interest thus ensuring an American sale for the book.

   Lawrence's Arabian nights (news item)
The Sunday Times (London), 13 March 1927

Lawrence: lies or legends?
Newsweek (New York), 15 February 1954, pp 100–2. illus
An article following on from the news of Aldington's book on Lawrence which came to light as a result of Aldington's negotiations with American publishers. It briefly recounts the Lawrence legend and, although Aldington was reluctant to discuss his manuscript, he was interviewed about the book. It, according to Aldington, began as 'a sympathetic study of a military hero' but 'I came to feel that Lawrence was only a legend, then a legend intentionally spread by himself with little or no regard for the truth. That's what my book is about: the legend of Lawrence, how it started and how it spread.'

The article also includes an interview with Lowell Thomas who claimed that Lawrence 'played a major role in the campaign in the Near East' but the main people who could substantiate the story were dead. 'As for me, I'm not dead and will defend Lawrence until I am.'

Lawrence's defenders
Newsweek (New York), 5 April 1954, pp 47–8
This article discusses the reactions of Lawrence's admirers to the news of Aldington's book. It discusses the actions of Liddell Hart, Kennington and Lord Winterton in trying to prevent Aldington from quoting from their works, and their readiness to contest any claims that he might be putting forward. The article also claims that Liddell Hart approached the publishers to try and stop publication but the request was refused.

Lloyd, L.
Seven Pillars of Wisdom (review)
National Review, September 1935, pp 342–6

Lovelock, R. C. O.
   The Mint and the metal: T. E. Lawrence's life in the RAF
Flight, 8 March 1955, p 356
A favourable review of *The Mint*

Lunt, J. D.
   An unsolicited tribute
Blackwood's Magazine, April 1955, pp 289–96
A contemporary account of a visit to the Hedjaz railway and interviews with Arabs who fought with Lawrence.

Mack, John E.
   The inner conflict of T. E. Lawrence
The Times (London), 8 February 1969, p 17

Mack, John E.
   T. E. Lawrence: a study of heroism and conflict
American Jnl of Psychiatry, 8 February 1969, pp 1083–92
Discusses at length the psychological problems of Lawrence's self-esteem and its effects upon his public actions.

Malraux, Andre
   Lawrence and the demon of the absolute
Hudson Review, Winter 1956, pp 519–32
A complex article centred on *The Seven Pillars of Wisdom*, not a critique, 'but an analysis of the feelings of the author in the presence of his book—feelings which are later to be modified'. At the outset Malraux maintains that Lawrence's resignation from the Colonial Office was to further one aim, that of making sense of the confusion of what had been his fate and this was to be achieved through *The Seven Pillars of Wisdom*. The commitment to the book was even more of a commitment than the Arab Revolt and Lawrence found himself 'imprisoned with the book for his decisive struggle with the angel'. Malraux faults the book for its lack of characterisation as the portrayal of the

Arabs 'scarcely went beyond the picturesque, that of the English beyond a crude sketch. What reader, the book closed, "knows" Joyce, Young, Clayton?'

Although the book had been written shortly after the capture of Damascus and rewritten after the loss of the manuscript, Malraux maintains that the book could not be completely rewritten as corrections would not have altered the perspective. 'Why would the demon that had already twice paralysed him have been defeated the third time? It was himself.' Throughout the book Malraux judges Lawrence to be constantly at odds with himself with 'under his pride, if not humility at least a powerful and spasmodic taste for self-humiliation, now by discipline and now by veneration; a horror of respectability; a disgust for possessions, for money, a disinterestedness which took for itself the form of clarity of heart; a thorough-going sense of his guilt, pursued by his angels or his minor demons, a sense of evil, and of the nothingness of almost everything that men cling to; a need for the absolute, an instinctive taste for asceticism'.

Malraux, Andre
The Quest of T. E. Lawrence
World Review, September/October 1949

Marsh, Edward
Number of people
Harper's Magazine, July 1939, pp 173-4
Includes reminiscences on Lawrence.

Mills, Gordon
T. E. Lawrence as a writer
Texas Quarterly, Vol 5, No 3, 1962, pp 34-45
This paper discusses Lawrence as a writer from an examination of *The Seven Pillars of Wisdom*. Mills considers Lawrence's style

of writing which he feels reveals a highly conscious control although it has been criticised, by Lawrence as well as others, as being too highly contrived and too literary though this fault can also be considered a virtue.

In discussing Lawrence's use of motifs, Mills feels that there are several discernible, some confined to individual chapters and others part of much larger units. The work can be considered as a work of history despite being a personal narrative, and Mills concludes that 'as with style, motif, and historiography, a direction can be discerned. It is not really so complex a book that it need escape a reasonable understanding. It deserves not to.'

Monkhouse, G.
Retreat: Clouds Hill
The Guardian (Manchester), 10 September 1963, p 7, illus

Mousa, Suleiman
The role of the Syrians and Iraqis in the Arab Revolt
Middle East Forum, Vol XLIII, No 1, 1967, pp 5–17
This article discusses Lawrence's claim that the Syrians and Iraqis had done nothing to bring about their freedom, which he first voiced in a letter to his family on 12 February 1917, writing: 'The time is not yet ripe to talk of Palestine, Syria and Iraq, for these three countries have made no attempt to liberate themselves, in spite of wholly favourable circumstances.' In *The Seven Pillars of Wisdom* he wrote that the Syrians 'looked outside for help, and expected freedom to come by entreaty, not by sacrifice'.

Mousa discusses the reasons for Lawrence's claim which he feels was based on two misconceptions, the first being the impression that the mass of the Arab peoples actively supported the Arab secret societies, and the second the failure of Iraq and Syria to rise in spontaneous revolt against the Turks. The article details the part played by the Syrians and Iraqis in the campaign against the Turks and concludes that the majority of Feisal's northern army were mainly Syrians and Iraqis—a force which provided powerful support for Allenby.

Mousa does, however, offer reasons as to why so many Iraqis and Syrians were not prepared to make any effort against the Turks and these are worth listing:

1   The authority of the Turks had been established through force of habit and lack of a national consciousness.
2   The strength of the religious link.
3   Local dissent amongst the Arabs. For example Ibn Rashid, Emir of Northern Nejd, supported the Turks because his enemy Ibn Saud, Emir of Southern Nejd at that time, supported the British.
4   Fear of war damage.

———

Mud on the White Robe
Times Educational Supplement, 4 February 1955
A review article based on Aldington's book.

Muggeridge, Malcolm
Poor Lawrence
New Statesman, 27 October 1961, pp 604–5
Review of *Lawrence of Arabia* by Anthony Nutting.

Newcombe, S. F.
T. E. Lawrence: Personal Reminiscences
Qtly Statement Palestine Exploration Fund, July 1935, pp 110–13
A brief summary of Lawrence's archaeological work for the Palestine Exploration Fund prior to World War I. At this time Newcombe was engaged on a mapping survey of Palestine which was to prove invaluable at a later date.

Nickerson, H.
  Lawrence and future generalship
American Review, December 1935, pp 129–54, maps
Deals extensively with Lawrence's military tactics.

Nicolson, Harold
  The Lawrence legend
The Observer (London), 30 January 1955
A review of Aldington's book.

Nonopoulos, James A.
  The tragic and the epic in T. E. Lawrence
Yale Review, Spring 1935, pp 331–45
The theme of this article is the relation between the epic as
presented by *The Seven Pillars of Wisdom* and the tragedy of
Lawrence's later life. A comparison is made between the *Seven
Pillars* and the *Odyssey* in its literary form and this is discussed
in relation to Lawrence's translation of the *Odyssey*. The description of the Arab Revolt by Lawrence is compared with the
Iliad, with Auda cast as the Homeric character 'imbued with
the sense of heroic genealogy even as we find in Hippolochos'
speech to Diomedes in the *Iliad*'. The author concludes that
attempts to understand Lawrence through the world of Freud
are futile as it fails to comprehend 'the personal price he paid,
the price of Greek heroes who are "bound hand and foot to
fatal destiny"'.

Perkins, G.
  The Arab Revolt—further light on Feisal and Lawrence
(letter)
Morning Post, 13 September 1933

Personal glimpses—wrecking Turkish trains with Lawrence of Arabia.
Literary Digest (USA), 19 March 1927

Philby, H. A. R.
Seven Pillars of Wisdom (review)
The Sunday Times, 28 July 1935

Philby, H. A. R.
Lawrence of Arabia: the work behind the legend
Review of Reviews (London), June 1935, pp 15–17, map
The main thread of this article is the discussion of the basic misconception, in Philby's view, of Lawrence and the Arab Bureau in supporting the Sherifian family instead of Ibn Saud. In 1914 Ibn Saud had already begun to harass the Turks and Philby felt that he, not Hussein, should have received support. Philby concludes by stating that the only monument to Lawrence's work were the destroyed remains of the Hedjaz railway. 'El Orens, Destroyer of Engines, as he was known to the Turks, earned his nickname.'
It should be borne in mind that Philby gave long and devoted service to Ibn Saud, and some of his views on the Sherifian family, although to a certain extent backed by subsequent events, are coloured by this relationship.

Powell, A.
Lawrence of Arabia
Punch, 2 February 1955
A review of Aldington's book

Preston, R. C.
The Mint (review)
Aeroplane, 18 March 1955, p 365

Prince, A. E.
Lawrence of Arabia
Queens Quarterly, Autumn 1935, pp 366–77
This appreciation of Lawrence provides a useful resumé of his career, his motives and his reactions to the peace settlement. It traces the growth of the legend which began after the Armistice and was fostered by Lowell Thomas's lecture tours and sustained by the appearance of *Revolt in the Desert*. The article briefly outlines his archaeological work, his military exploits, his relations with Hussein and his military tactics which made Liddell Hart class Lawrence 'among the supreme captains of all time on account of his exposition of the art of war, grounded on a wide range of military studies, notably the work of eighteenth century strategists'. Prince feels that Lawrence's subsequent actions were of no surprise to his friends as he was merely using the ranks of the Army and Air Force as a substitute for the monastic life of the Middle Ages. 'Lawrence had a portion of the spirit of Aristophanes, compact with that of Malory's Sir Galahad.'

Pritchett, V. S.
Ross at the Depot
New Statesman, 18 February 1955
Review of *The Mint*.

Pritchett, V. S.
Self-portrait of the author from selected writings
New Statesman, 28 April 1951, p 480
A review of *The Essential T. E. Lawrence*, edited by David Garnett, which Pritchett feels succeeds in presenting a self-portrait of Lawrence rather than a representation of his writings for their own sake. The review examines the extracts to try to ascertain the portrait that the writings convey, and Pritchett discerns a portrait which is of 'merciless mental energy which

pours out endlessly in words or action and turns upon the character with humiliating self-criticism. There is the special kind of idealism: ascetic, bodiless, rational, unromantic, and it keeps a place for the inevitable cynicism of tactics.'

Quigly, I.
A kind of hero: Lawrence of Arabia
The Spectator, 14 December 1962, p 933
A favourable review of the film *Lawrence of Arabia*, with an introduction analysing the reasons for the questioning of the Lawrence legend.

Rattigan, C.
Lawrence the soldier
Saturday Review, 31 March 1934, p 350, portrait

Read, Herbert
The Seven Pillars of Wisdom
The Bibliophile's Almanack, 1928, pp 35-41
This review deals with Lawrence's book from two viewpoints, the first being the physical presentation of the work which Read deplores, describing it as 'a monstrous exhibition of all that a book should not be'. Read considers the content by posing the question 'who is the hero of the story: Colonel Lawrence or the Arabian army?' and concludes that if the former then the story does not reach epic qualities and if the latter then one cannot fail to overlook 'the overwhelming venality, pettiness, fanaticism and ignorance of the mass of them' with their contribution being 'no more than a dance of flies in the air beside the magnitude of that earthly conflict' which was represented by the real war on the Western Front.

Read ends by comparing *Seven Pillars* with Doughty's *Arabia Deserta* and concludes that Lawrence's book is not in the same category and by implication neither can the two men be compared.

The reluctant money spinner
The Times (London), 9 January 1971, p 15, illus
A review of Howard's book, *Jonathan Cape, Publisher* (see p 96),
which deals with Lawrence's association with the firm. The
review deals mainly with the publication of *The Seven Pillars
of Wisdom* and *Revolt in the Desert*, both of which were important books as far as the fortunes of Cape were concerned.

Review of *The Mint*
Blackwoods Magazine, April 1955, pp 382–4
An unfavourable review.

Revolt in the Desert (review)
Illustrated London News, 12 March 1927, p 432, illus

Revolt in the Desert (review)
New Statesman, 12 March 1927, pp 668–9

Revolt in the Desert (review)
Saturday Review, 12 March 1927, pp 426–7

Rhode, E.
Two and a half pillars of wisdom
The Listener, 20 December 1962, p 1055, illus
An unfavourable review of the film *Lawrence of Arabia*.

Roberts, Chalmers
Lawrence of Arabia: A Mystification—An Impression—A
Tribute
The World Today, April 1927, pp 441–5
A very favourable article on Lawrence which deals briefly with

his career in the Middle East, the problems of settling down after the Peace Settlement and the writing of *The Seven Pillars of Wisdom* and *Revolt in the Desert.*

Rollo, C. J.
Book with a past (review of *The Mint*)
Atlantic Monthly, May 1935, p 82

———

Ross, by T. Rattigan (criticism)
Educational Theatre Jnl, March 1962, pp 66-7

———

Ross, by T. Rattigan (criticism)
Hudson Review, Spring 1962, p 117

Rosselli, John
The Devil's Advocate
Manchester Guardian, 1 February 1955
Review of Aldington's book.

Rosselli, John
Was T. E. Lawrence a fake?
The Reporter, 21 April 1955, pp 49-52
This article tries to look at the Lawrence legend after the initial outburst which followed the publication of Aldington's biographical inquiry on Lawrence, illustrating some of the points made by Aldington and the counter claims of the 'Lawrence Bureau', as Aldington named those who supported Lawrence's claims.

No real conclusions are made as to whether Lawrence was a fake but the point is made that Aldington had not provided the real picture of Lawrence because Lawrence '. . . fought coherence. I could not and cannot do for him what he had set against doing for himself' (Robert Graves). The writer feels that probably the best assessment was that expressed by C. M. Woodhouse when he commented on Aldington's book as follows: 'Aldington in a muddled and savage way has helped to show what Lawrence was not; but he has not shown what Lawrence was, and he has made it harder for others to find out.'

Sacher, Howard M.

The Declining world of T. E. Lawrence
New Republic, 10 May 1954, pp 18–19
This article was prompted by the pre-publication evidence presented by Aldington to substantiate the view that the Lawrence legend was a deliberate fabrication. The article was written prior to the book being published and does not attempt to evaluate the exploits of Lawrence but the world which he described as part of the legend, not from the military viewpoint, 'but also the nobility with which he invested the Arab World'.

Sacher feels that the contemporary reporters, who painted a picture of the Arabs that was far divorced from the world of *Arabia Deserta* and T. E. Lawrence, presented a more accurate picture of a world 'savagely exploited by Communists and Fundamentalist propagandists, manoeuvred for dynastic purposes by the calculating Hashemites'. Although the deep-rooted hunger for freedom existed it was 'but one slender strand in a larger tapestry of corruption and reaction; it is not the brilliant magic carpet on which T. E. Lawrence rode into battle'.

Sandall, R.

Lawrence of Arabia (review of film)
Film Quarterly, Spring 1963, pp 56–7, illus

Scawen, W.

The romantic as a man of action
Adelphi, Vol 27, No 4, 1951, pp 330–3

Review of *The Essential T. E. Lawrence*, selected by David Garnett.

_____

Seven Pillars of Wisdom (review)
The Times (London), 29 July 1935

_____

Seven Pillars of Wisdom (review)
Illustrated London News, 17 August 1935, p 276

_____

Seven Pillars of Wisdom (review)
The Times Literary Supplement, August 1935, p 487

_____

Seven Pillars of Wisdom: publications plans (news item)
The Times (London), 31 May 1935

Shaw, G. B.
Revolt in the Desert (review)
The Spectator, 12 March 1927, p 429

Sheean, V.
Ear to the RAF
Saturday Review, 2 April 1955, pp 20–1
Review of *The Mint*.

_____

Solitary in the Ranks (review of *The Mint*)
The Times (London), 17 February 1955

_____

The Solitary Warrior
Times Literary Supplement, 1 June 1951, p 340
Article on *The Essential T. E. Lawrence*, selected by David Garnett.

Squire, J.
   Lawrence of Arabia: a biographical enquiry (review)
Illustrated London News, 12 February 1955, pp 224–6, illus
A critical review of Aldington's book.

Stirling, W. F.
   Tales of Lawrence of Arabia
Cornhill Magazine, April 1933, pp 495–510
An interesting account of some of Lawrence's exploits in the
Arab Revolt from an intelligence officer who served with him
from 1918 onwards. Stirling provides accounts of raids against
the Turks and these testify to the physical endurance of Lawrence and the effectiveness of his tactics. He also provides an
entertaining portrait of Auda, chieftain of the Abu Tayi branch
of the Howeitat tribe, who nicknamed Lawrence the 'Imp of the
World' which Stirling consideres to be '. . . about the most apt
and terse description of him that has ever been given'. The
article ends by posing the question 'Why cannot the Government employ him?' and by answering it with the view that
Lawrence would not accept a job if it were offered. 'But all the
same it is a thousand pities that when a genius is given to the
world it so often happens that the world does not realise the
true value of such a gift.'

Storrs, Ronald
   Charles Doughty and T. E. Lawrence
The Listener, 25 December 1947

Storrs, Ronald
   Lawrence of Arabia: abstract
Great Britain and the East, 25 January 1940, p 61
An abstract of a lecture on Lawrence given by Storrs at the
French Institute on 17 January 1940. It outlines Lawrence's
harassing tactics against the Turks, his poor knowledge of

Arabic and his ascendancy over the Bedouin by sheer willpower and physical effort.

Storrs, Ronald
  Lawrence of Arabia: a review of Richard Aldington's book
The Listener, 3 February 1955, pp 187-9
A highly critical examination of Aldington's work.

Storrs, Ronald
  Maurice Baring and T. E. Lawrence
English, Vol VIII, No 45, Autumn 1950, pp 112-16
An article concerning an anthology of poems presented to Lawrence by Maurice Baring in 1929. It was, according to Storrs, greatly treasured by Lawrence and was being used by him at Clouds Hill prior to his death. After Lawrence's death the collection was entrusted to Storrs by A. W. Lawrence.

Strauss, Ralph
  Revolt in the Desert (review)
The Sunday Times, 13 March 1927

Sugarman, Sidney
  The truth about T. E. Lawrence and the Arab Revolt
Jewish Observer and Middle East Review, 12 September 1969, pp 17-20
An examination of Lawrence and the Arab Revolt which concludes that the Arab Revolt was only a small part of the war and that its importance had been inflated because of Lawrence's writings and his active encouragement of the Lowell Thomas lectures. In considering the political problems of the Middle East before and after the revolt, Sugarman considers that 'It is hardly surprising that we now have a Middle East consumed by hatreds and frustrations and a deep, relentless urge to wipe out imagined wrongs and fictitious injustices with blood'.

Sykes, Christopher
Mystery motorist
The Spectator, 20 July 1962, p 89
A review of *Letters to T. E. Lawrence*, edited by A. W. Lawrence.
The main criticism of the work is the lack of quotation from
Lawrence's side of the correspondence, which would have given
a balanced picture.

Symonds, J.
The lost heroes: T. E. Lawrence
The Sunday Times Magazine, 29 January 1967, p 23, illus

———

T. E. Lawrence: an effigy in Wareham Church, Dorset
Builder, 22 March 1940, pp 354, 359, illus

Thespis
Ross, by T. Rattigan (criticism)
English, Spring 1961, p 148

Toynbee, Philip
Lawrence into Ross
The Observer (London), 13 February 1955
A review of *The Mint*

Trewin, J. W.
Ross, by T. Rattigan (criticism)
Illustrated London News, 28 May 1960, p 944

———

Unpublished letters of Lawrence of Arabia
National Review, 10 September 1963, pp 203–5

———

Vanished Galahads
Time (New York), 30 August 1956, pp 54–5, illus
A review of *The Home Letters of T. E. Lawrence and His Brothers*

which considers the letters to be, in the main, very dull and not at all the sort of writing one would expect from a leader of men. The review lays particular stress on Lawrence's idealism which was pushed to 'a limit where it became almost inhuman—divorced from instinct and passion, too cold for natural comfort, almost too good to be true'. This point is also made by Churchill in the preface in which he likened Lawrence to a 'dweller upon the mountain top where the air is cold, crisp, rarefied, and where the view on clear days commands all the kingdoms of the world and the glory of them'.

Vansittart, Lord
The Lawrence legend
Daily Telegraph, 31 January 1955
A review of Aldington's work.

Villard, Oswald Garrison
Issues and men: Colonel Lawrence
Nation, 19 June 1935, p 703
This obituary of Lawrence begins by posing the unanswered questions asked about Lawrence at that time and by suggesting that as long as the story of World War I was still being written 'the romantic mystery of Lawrence will be studied, rewritten, reworked until it grows more and more into mythology'. The writer, whilst recognising Lawrence's planning of his campaign and his development of irregular warfare, abhorred the ruthless slaughter that accompanied his campaigns, especially when he allowed his irregulars to get out of hand and to slaughter defenceless prisoners, women and children.

Vogler, Lewis
Poet of the Arab sands
Saturday Review of Literature, 16 October 1954, p 21
A review of *The Home Letters of T. E. Lawrence and His Brothers*

which considers Lawrence's letters to have been 'even more than in the case of many other writers, . . . literary exercise' and show him to be a worthy follower of Burton, Kinglake and, in particular, Doughty. The section of letters from Carchemish are considered to be the best, revealing his interest in archaeology, his growing knowledge of Arabia and his love of artifacts. The reviewer finds Lawrence a complex personality and 'It is difficult to read even a few of the letters without an awareness of his sharpness of spirit . . . he was, as a writer, almost incapable of dullness—even in his letters home'.

Warner, Oliver
Scott, Lawrence and the myth of British decadence
National Review, September 1941, pp 314–17
This article discusses the effect that Scott and Lawrence had on the Continental theory that Britain had become decadent, and although in a sense both men had failed, they had risen above their failures 'for which they themselves could not be held responsible, and helped to work a spiritual miracle for the health of their country'.

In reading this article it should be remembered that it was written during a bleak period in World War II and as a result the sentiments are extremely patriotic.

Weintraub, Stanley
Bernard Shaw's other St. Joan
South Atlantic Qtly, Spring 1965, pp 194–205
An interesting article in which Weintraub discusses the hypothesis that Lawrence may have unconsciously been a model for Shaw's *St Joan* resulting from the contact and friendship between the two men whilst the play was being written. (For further details of the friendship see Weintraub's *Private Shaw and Public Shaw*, p 121.)

At the time that Shaw was writing his play he was also reading Lawrence's Oxford edition of *Seven Pillars*, and according to visitors, was much taken by its content and style, feeling that Lawrence had written one of the era's great books. Weintraub contends that 'Whether the coincidences helped shape the play and its preface can only be surmised, but striking parallels are there and perhaps represent Shavian perspectives upon the legendary Maid and the living legend of the ascetic former knight of the desert'.

Weintraub draws other parallels between Shaw's *St Joan* and Lawrence, citing as examples their military tactics, their habit of dressing as their soldiers dressed, their brushes with official-dom and their attitudes to sex and physical contact. Weintraub feels that the similarities may not have been evident either to Shaw or Lawrence but that instead of Shaw inscribing a copy to Lawrence with the words 'To Pte Shaw from Public Shaw' he might have written 'To Bernard Shaw's other *St Joan*'.

Weintraub, Stanley
  Lawrence of Arabia (review of film)
  Film Qtly, Spring 1964, pp 51, illus

Wheeler, K.
  Romantic riddle of Lawrence of Arabia
  Life, 21 January 1962, pp 94–102

Wilkinson, C.
  Revolt in the Desert (review)
  London Mercury, May 1927, pp 62–9

Williams, Kenneth
  The strange self-told tale of T. E. Lawrence
  Great Britain and the East, 1 December 1938, p 597
  A brief article which considers the romantic riddle of Lawrence and its imperfections but which feels that the letters of Lawrence show another side of his character, that of a man born out of his

time. The writer feels that Lawrence's actions after the revolt were those of a seeker who 'went to his death unsatisfied. But he went with courage and with no illusions.'

Wilson, A. T.
Revolt in the Desert (review)
Jnl Central Asian Society, 14, 1927, pp 282–5
A highly critical review of the book by a Political Officer who was in Mesopotamia during the Arab Revolt and in common with others who were attached to the India Office he was highly critical of the work of the Arab Bureau.

Woodhouse, C. M.
T. E. Lawrence: New legends for old
Twentieth Century, March 1955, pp 228–36
A reasoned examination of Aldington's book and the whole approach to the Lawrence legend.

Woolf, L.
Revolt in the Desert (review)
Nation, 19 March 1927, p 857

Yeats-Brown, F.
Lawrence as I knew him
The Spectator, 24 May 1935, pp 872–3
This article is concerned mainly with Lawrence's association with Yeats-Brown in his capacity as Assistant Editor of the *Spectator*. Lawrence undertook reviewing work for that journal using the pseudonym 'C.D.' and when asked why he remained in the Air Force when he could earn a good living from writing, Lawrence replied 'I draw four bob a day: two whole pennies for every hour I live, even when I'm asleep: that's enough for me'.

Lawrence was constantly apologising for the quality of his prose and his style when writing for the journal, and Yeats-Brown felt that Lawrence's writing had flaws of 'jarring sentences, complications, obscurities, a straining for effect' but in spite of these defects his writings would live 'because they are symbolical of the grandeur and misery of his time and because through them and in them shines the greatness of the man'.

Zinar, H. D.
Damaging self-portrait of T. E. Lawrence (review of *The Mint*)
Daily Telegraph, 18 February 1955

Zinnser, William K.
In search of Lawrence of Arabia
Esquire, June 1961, pp 101–4
This article was motivated by the play *Ross* which was running in London at that time and due to open on Broadway, and the projected Sam Spiegel-David Lean film on Lawrence. The article begins by surveying Lawrence's career from his compilation of his thesis in 1909 to his death in 1935 and in particular, the 'legend' as created by Lowell Thomas and furthered by Robert Graves and Liddell Hart. At first Lawrence entered into the legend but 'recoiled in horror from the results. It was alright for the public to see the legend as long as they didn't see him.'

The legend was rekindled by the play and the film and the article examines the play and the projected film. Spiegel felt that Lawrence was a good subject for a film because he was 'a man in conflict with his destiny. What excites me about this picture is its contradictions. They are responsible for the legend and they will be responsible for a good movie.' The author feels that, if nothing else, the play and film would give the legend new life and that a new generation would find 'something uniquely hypnotic in the name of "Lawrence of Arabia"'.

Section E

General works on the Middle East War with relevant references to Lawrence

Bell, Gertrude
'The Arab War'

THE ARAB WAR | CONFIDENTIAL INFORMATION FOR | GENERAL HEADQUARTERS FROM.| GERT- RUDE BELL | BEING DESPATCHES REPRINTED FROM | THE SECRET 'ARAB BULLETIN' | Introduction by | Sir KINAHAN CORNWALLIS | KCMG, CBE, DSO | Director of the Arab Bureau | 1916-20 | THE GOLDEN COCKEREL PRESS |

1L + pp (1)–52 + 1L.

Contents:
These articles were written by Gertrude Bell between October 1916 and July 1917 for the Arab Bureau in Cairo and were pub- lished in the *Arab Bulletin* which was the secret intelligence summary of the Bureau (see also Secret Despatches from Arabia p 45). Its importance lies in the background information that it provides, complementing the work of Lawrence for the Bureau and giving an informed picture of the situation in the Middle East at that time.

Benoist-Mechin, Jacques
'Arabian Destiny,' by Jacques Benoist-Mechin
London: Elek Books, 1957

x, 298pp, illus, maps, bibl, index, 21cm.

A brief survey of the history of the Arab peoples ending with the death of Ibn Saud in 1953. This is of interest as it presents the French view of events especially in relation to British support of the Sherifian family and the neglect of Ibn Saud.

Bonsal, Stephen
'Suitors and Supplicants', by Stephen Bonsal, with an introduction by Arthur Krock
New York: Prentice-Hall Inc, 1946

xvi, 301pp, app, index, 23cm.

The author was attached to the Peace Conference in Paris and this is an account of the arguments and pleas presented by the small nations, including the Arab States. The section covering the Arab case appears on pp 32–51. A further reference to Lawrence appears in the chapter devoted to the Zionist case (pp 56–7).

Boyle, Andrew
'Trenchard', by Andrew Boyle
London: Collins, 1962

768pp, illus, maps

The biography of the man who played a considerable part in Lawrence's association with the Air Force, smoothing over his initial problem in joining, and furthering his re-admission to the ranks after his brief spell in the Royal Tank Corps. Trenchard and Lawrence became friends in 1921; the friendship was strengthened by the feelings that both men had for the Air Force, which was still in its infancy and often under pressure from the politicians. It became a standing joke between them that Lawrence was 'helping to build your service from below'.

Bray, Major N. N. E.
'Shifting Sands', 1934

MAJOR N. N. E. BRAY | (rule) | SHIFTING SANDS | *Foreword by* | THE RIGHT HONOURABLE | SIR AUSTEN CHAMBERLAIN, KG, MP, | LONDON | (rule) | UNICORN PRESS |

1L + pp (i)–xii, pp 1–312, 21½cm.

1L, blank; verso, Map of Arabia; pp (i), Half-title; verso, blank; Frontispiece; pp (iii), Title-page; verso, First Published November, 1934 etc; pp v–vi, Foreword; pp vii–viii, List of Contents; pp ix–x, List of Illustrations; pp xi–xii, Preface; pp 1–7, Prologue; pp 8–304, Text; pp 305–12, Index.

The author served with the Indian Army before seeing service in Arabia. In his prologue, Bray states that he wrote his book because of pressure from others who had taken part in the Arab Revolt, and because a distorted view of the Arab Revolt had been presented to the public by earlier books.

He is critical of the Arab Revolt and its leaders and, more especially Lawrence's guerrilla tactics, which Bray felt were secondary to the real military objectives. He also criticises Lawrence's political activities, especially his concealment from the

Arabs of the Anglo-French agreement on what was to happen to the Middle East on the termination of hostilities.

Bray, N. N. E.
'A Paladin of Arabia': The Biography of Brevet Lieut-Colonel G. E. Leachman, of the Royal Sussex Regiment, by N. N. E. Bray
London: John Heritage, 1936

xvi, 429pp, illus, maps, 20cm.

Although this work is not really connected with Lawrence it is worthy of inclusion because of Leachman's work in Mesopotamia. It is essential to a complete understanding of the situation in the Middle East at the time of the Arab Revolt, that one also considers events in Mesopotamia and these are inseparable from Leachman.

As a political agent, Leachman played a large part in establishing Britain's position in Mesopotamia especially in the light of the disastrous events that led up to the siege at Kut. (It was at this siege that Lawrence tried to ransom the besieged garrison.) During the revolt in Mesopotamia, Leachman played an important role in its control and settlement though his actions and those of the other political officers involved Lawrence's wrath in *The Times*. Bray considers Lawrence's condemnation unjustified as he knew very little of the situation in Mesopotamia and also because the unrest was being fermented by extremists from Syria using Feisal's money which originally came from the British Government.

Brodrick, Alan Houghton
'Near to Greatness: A Life of the Sixth Earl Winterton',
by Alan Houghton Brodrick
London: Hutchinson, 1965

272pp, frontis, illus, refs, index, 21½cm.

References to Lawrence: pp 17, 18, 177–83, 185.

A biography of one of Lawrence's companion officers during the Arab Revolt.

Falls, Cyril
'Armageddon 1918', by Cyril Falls
London: Weidenfeld & Nicolson, 1964

x, 216pp, illus, maps, notes, bibl, index, 21½cm.

(Great Battles of History Series)

This work deals with the war in the Middle East and has numerous references to Lawrence. It gives a straightforward account of the campaign and Lawrence's part in this. Falls writes: 'He was a brilliant but unorthodox natural soldier and later became a great writer. His narratives must, however, be accepted with caution, since he occasionally exaggerated without shame or scruple.'

Gardner, Brian
'Allenby', by Brian Gardner
London: Cassell, 1965

xx, 314pp, illus, maps, notes, index, 21½cm.

References to Lawrence: pp ix, xiv–xv, xvii–xviii, 13, 117, 129, 131–2, 135–44, 151–2, 158–9, 162, 165, 169, 171, 178, 182, 187–91, 200–11, 224, 227, 229, 238–9, 260, 264, 269–71, 273–4.

A most important work, as much of Lawrence's success stemmed from Allenby's arrival in Egypt. The biography deals with the relationship between the two men and also with the way that Lawrence's actions fitted into Allenby's general plans for the Arabian campaign. It is also an attempt to redress the balance and to show that the overshadowing of Allenby was an historical mistake.

Graves, Philip P. (editor)
'Memoirs of King Abdullah of Transjordan', edited by Philip P. Graves, with an introduction by R. J. C. Broadhurst
London: Jonathan Cape, 1950

278pp, illus, refs, app, index, 20½cm.

References to Lawrence: pp 18, 23, 91, 157ff, 165ff, 170ff, 200ff, 225.

An interesting work, representing the viewpoint of the son of Sherif Hussein, leader of the Arab Revolt. It is also of value for the Arab view of the campaign and the political intrigues which preceded and followed the revolt against Turkey.

Howarth, David
'The Desert King: A Life of Ibn Saud', by David Howarth
London: Collins, 1964

252pp, illus, bibl, index, 21cm.

References to Lawrence: pp 73, 78, 80, 87, 90–9, 100, 102, 104, 106, 108, 133, 147, 174.

The biography of Ibn Saud, the Arab leader who was ignored by the Allies in preference to the Sherifian family. Despite the reasons for the choice of Hussein as Britain's ally in the campaign, mainly his position as Sherif of Mecca and his sons' contact with prominent Arabs in Syria, Howarth considers the ignoring of Ibn Saud an error that was proved by the aftermath of the peace settlement.

Although the biography has little to do directly with Lawrence, its value lies in the way in which Howarth sets out the reasons for the trouble between the Sherifian family and Ibn Saud, not the least of which was the religious question. Ib Saud was the leader of a religious movement which pursued Islam in its disciplined form and he regarded Hussein and his family as decadent and unfit custodians of the Holy City of Mecca, a situation that he rectified in 1924 with the taking of Mecca by force.

This is an extremely readable biography which provides the reader with the remainder of the picture in the Middle East prior to, and subsequent to the Middle East War. Another biography of interest is *Lord of Arabia* by H. C. Armstrong (Barker, 1934) which also deals with Ibn Saud.

Jarvis, C. S.
'Arab Command': The biography of Lieutenant-Colonel F. W. Peake Pasha, by Major C. S. Jarvis
London: Hutchinson, 1942

158pp, frontis, illus, index, 22cm.

References to Lawrence: pp 9, 24, 26, 29–36, 39–40, 42–3, 45–54, 78, 80–6, 93, 95, 134, 151, 153.

The biography of one of the officers who served with Lawrence during the Arab Revolt and later in Transjordan with the Arab Legion. It deals with Peake's part in the revolt and presents the view of one of Lawrence's officers both towards Lawrence and the Arabs. The work also deals with the post-war problems in Arabia and with Lawrence's work as adviser to the Colonial Office.

Kedourie, Elie
'England and the Middle East': The Destruction of the Ottoman Empire 1914–21, by Elie Kedourie
London: Bowes & Bowes, 1956

viii, 9–236pp, app, bibl, index, 21cm.

An interesting work which deals with the destruction of the Ottoman Empire in detail after a brief introduction which sets the scene from 1830–1914. The book deals solely with the involvement of Britain in the Middle East through the crucial period from the Sykes-Picot agreement through to the troubles in Mesopotamia after the war. In the chapter which deals with Lawrence, the author attempts to analyse Lawrence's motives and concludes that these were known only to Lawrence and were a part of his personal problems which he pursued with a passionate conviction. He also discusses Lawrence's association with Feisal, his antagonism towards the French and the implications of the Sykes-Picot agreement in his dealings with the Arabs. Kedourie concludes that Lawrence was a manipulator of events using whatever explanations suited his actions, however damaging they were to the cause he served: '. . . he would see where his possibilities might lead, but he was under no illusions as to the significance of the experiment. To the clear-sighted, failure was the only goal.'

Kedourie, Elie
'The Chatham House Version and Other Middle-Eastern Studies', by Elie Kedourie
London: Weidenfeld & Nicolson, 1970

(viii), 488pp, notes, bibl, index, 22cm.

This work consists of a collection of studies dealing with the political history of the Middle East. Although many of the studies are only of fringe interest, they do provide an excellent backcloth to the Middle East from the turn of the century. Of particular importance is the study on the Capture of Damascus on pp 33-47, followed by a precis of the Australian War Diaries on which the study is based. This study discusses the question of the fall of Damascus in relation to Lawrence's claim that it was captured by the Sherifian forces which Kedourie maintains is an inaccurate version. (See Prefatory Essay, p 20.)

Kirkbride, Alec Seath
'A Crackle of Thorns', by Sir Alec Seath Kirkbride
London: John Murray, 1956

(viii), 201pp, illus, index, 22cm.

References to Lawrence: pp 2, 5-11.

Mention of Lawrence is mainly of a superficial nature and related to the author's contact with him during the Arab Revolt. The rest of the work is useful for the picture it gives of the post-1919 developments in the Middle East.

MacMunn, George, and Falls, Cyril (compilers)
'History of the Great War', Military Operations Egypt
and Palestine from the outbreak of war with Germany to
June 1917, compiled by Lieut-General Sir George
MacMunn and Captain Cyril Falls
London: HMSO, 1928

xviii, 445pp, illus, maps, refs, app, indexes, 22½cm.

References to Lawrence: pp 233 (footnote), 235–6, 239–40.

MacMunn, George, and Becke, A. F. (compilers)
'History of the Great War', Military Operations Egypt
and Palestine from June 1917 to the end of the war, com-
piled by George MacMunn and A. F. Becke
London: HMSO, 1930, in two parts

Part 1: xxiii, 394pp + xiv, illus, maps, refs, glossary, 22½cm.
Part 2: 395–748pp, illus, maps, app, indexes (parts 1 & 2).

References to Lawrence: Parts 2 & 3 (indexed together), pp 260, 398, 400, 402, 404–6, 563, 565, 582–3, 585, 591.

This work is an official history of the war and contains several references to Lawrence. It is of value to the reader for the general background it provides and because it places the Arab revolt in perspective.

Nicolson, Harold
'Peacemaking 1919', by Harold Nicolson
London: Methuen, 1964

xxiv, 378pp, index, 21½cm.

References to Lawrence: pp 141–2.

References to Lawrence are very brief and are limited to his attendance on Feisal at the Peace Conference. The work has been included in this bibliography because of the insight that it gives into the conference and the important bearing that this had on later developments in the Middle East.

Philby, H. St John
'Arabian Days', by H. St John Philby
London: Hale, 1948

xvi, 336pp, illus, index, 24cm.

An autobiography which preceded his book *Forty Years in the Wilderness* which deals in greater detail with Lawrence. This work does, however, have numerous references to Lawrence and provides a useful backcloth to the Middle East during the Arab Revolt and the political problems that followed the peace settlement. Of particular interest is the fact that the two men took different standpoints with Lawrence supporting the Sherifian family, and Philby supporting Ibn Saud.

Philby, H. St John
'Forty Years in the Wilderness', by H. St John Philby
London: Hale, 1957

xvi, 272pp, illus, maps, index, 23½cm.

References to Lawrence: pp 51, 73–4, 79, 82–109, 251.

This work assumes an importance when one considers that Philby was opposed to Lawrence's political support for the Sherifian family and would therefore be expected to criticise

Lawrence's part in the Arab Revolt. In fact Philby praises his contribution to the Revolt and in a consideration of Aldington's book says that his defence of Lawrence 'was provoked by what I regarded as a shameful attack on his memory and reputation'.

Philby is of course noted for his work with Ibn Saud, but for a time he worked with Lawrence when he took over from Lawrence as Chief British Representative in Transjordan in 1921. Although Lawrence was not an administrator, he was effective and his departure from Transjordan was a loss to Philby as 'He knows and is known to everybody in these parts; and many of them have been intimately associated with him for years during the military operations he conducted up and down the railway. That he has effected a great change in the situation since he came here two months ago admits of no doubt. He has turned a pessimistic outlook into one which admits of no doubt, the administration which he encouraged to function is working smoothly.'

In considering Lawrence as an individual, Philby contends that it was not his charm which carried him to the forefront but the 'fact that Lawrence was a genius, nothing more and nothing less, and therefore not to be judged or analysed by the standards applicable to more normal persons, however competent or distinguished'. Philby concludes that history will probably show, as Aldington said, that 'Lawrence was the appropriate hero of his class and epoch' but that 'he might have added that it was a class and time which witnessed and survived the greatest cataclysm in the recorded history of man'.

Shane, Leslie
'Mark Sykes: His life and letters', by Leslie Shane, with an introduction by The Right Hon Winston Churchill
London: Cassell & Co, 1923

(xii), 308pp, illus, app, index, 23cm.

Although the references to Lawrence are brief, this is an important contribution to an understanding of the situation in the Middle East in relation to the Sykes-Picot agreement which laid the foundations of further unrest in the area. The author defends Sykes for the agreement which was determined by his brief from the Foreign Office, and for the fact that the agreement was an honest one compared with the other treaties imposed by the Paris Conference. 'He was influenced by two principles. His hatred of oppression urged him to do all in his power for the Arabs, the Jews, and the minor nationalities, while his loyalty to our Allies made him feverishly anxious not to betray the trust that the Parisian Press clamorously asserted that France reposed in us.'

Wavell, A. P.
'The Palestine Campaigns', by A. P. Wavell
London: Constable & Co, 3rd ed, 1938

xvi, 259pp, maps, app, index, 21cm.

References to Lawrence: pp 38, 54–6, 179, 199, 201, 203, 225, 229, 235, 250–1.

An excellent account of the Palestine campaigns which appeared as one in a series 'Campaigns and their lessons'. It stresses the value of the Arab Revolt to the Allies as it diverted Turkish reinforcements to the Hedjaz and protected the right flank of the British army. The revolt also acted as a counterbalance to the German propaganda machine which was operating in Persia, Afghanistan and Arabia.

The space devoted to the Arab Revolt is limited but it probably reflects its true place when the campaign is considered as a whole. Despite the lack of detailed coverage of the Arab Revolt, it is stressed that the Revolt was of great value to the Allied armies in defeating the Turks.

Woolley, Charles Leonard
'As I Seem to Remember', by Charles Leonard Woolley
London: Allen & Unwin, 1962

113pp, illus, 19cm.

A lighthearted collection of recollections which contains some interesting sidelights on Lawrence's and Woolley's archaeological work, especially in relation to their dealings with the Turks and the Germans.

Woolley, Charles Leonard
'Dead Towns and Living Men': being pages from an Antiquary's notebook, by Charles Leonard Woolley
London: Cape, 1932

(viii), 308pp, 20cm.

(The Life and Letters Series No 29. Originally published by OUP, 1920).

References to Lawrence: pp 74–177.

An interesting account of Lawrence's early work in the Middle East in the field of archaeology. It presents a very readable account of the difficulties faced by the two archaeologists in their dealings with the Turkish authorities, German engineers and the Arabs.

Young, Hubert
'The Independent Arab', by Major Sir Hubert Young
London: John Murray, 1933

xi, 344pp, maps, index, 22½cm.

Several references to Lawrence throughout the book.

An authoritative work by an officer who served in the Arab Revolt and who was closely involved in the peace negotiations and the troubles which followed the peace conference of 1920. Young became a British adviser to King Feisal of Iraq under High Commissioner Sir Percy Cox.

Section F

Arabic Sources on Lawrence

Abdullah El Hussein
'Memoirs of the King Abdullah El Hussein', introduced
and edited by Mustaffah Hajkh
Beirut: 1965

329pp, illus.

Al-Ghussein, Fa'iz
'My Memoirs of the Arab Revolt'
Damascus: Ibn Zaidun Press, 1939

272pp, 22cm.

The author was a member of Feisal's army from the declaration
of the revolt to the entry of the Allied forces into Damascus.
Before this he had been a constant threat to the Turkish authorities and had been imprisoned three times before being exiled to
Diar Bakr, whence he fled to India, returning before Feisal's
declaration of war.

Al-Jezairi, Amir Said Abdul Kader
'Jihad Nisf Qarn' (Struggle of half a century), edited by
Anwar al-Rifai'
Damascus: nd

292pp.

These memoirs deal with the Arab Revolt in general and the
part played by Lawrence. They also deal extensively with the
incident concerning the Algerians in Damascus; this incident
merely brought into the open the old rivalries which the Arab
Revolt had temporarily papered over.

189

Antonious, George
'The Arab Awakening': The story of the Arab national movement, by George Antonious
London: Hamish Hamilton, 1938

471pp, maps, app, index, 21cm.

References to Lawrence: pp 132, 211, 215–17, 221–2, 224, 283–4, 316–17, 319–24, 331–2, 369, 437.

An important work, as it is the first attempt to assess the Arab Revolt using both Arab and Western sources. The general assessment of Lawrence in this book is that his military services 'are spoken of with unfeigned admiration and gratitude throughout the Arab world. On the political side, the value of his contribution is questioned.' The general reader will find that the beginning of this book is extremely useful as it puts the Arab Revolt into its historical perspective commencing with Mohammed Ali in Egypt in 1811, and continuing through the gradual decline of the Ottoman Empire to the outbreak of war in 1914.

The second part of the book deals with the tentative beginnings of the Arab Revolt and Britain's pledges to the Arabs, especially the McMahon note of 24 October 1915 which has been used by the Arabs 'as the main piece of evidence on which the Arabs accuse Great Britain of having broken faith with them'. The work concludes with an account of the Arab Revolt and the post-war settlements, concentrating mainly on the political aspects. Although the book is very much an expression of the Arab viewpoint, it does provide a basis from which one can attempt to balance the differing approaches to the Arab Revolt and the part played by Lawrence and other British officers. Later Arab authorities have, however, disputed Antonious's

premise that the Arab Nationalist Movement began with Mohammed Ali but this does not detract from the value of the book,
especially in connection with the Arab Revolt.

**'The Arabic Revolution: Its Causes and Results', by one
of the members of the Arab Committee 1916
Cairo: 1916**

118pp, 29cm.

This work sets out to put the Arab Revolt into perspective by
discussing the Eastern problem in general, the Arab problem in
particular, and the relationship between the Arabs and the
Turks, concluding with the Arab Revolt.

**El Habtah, H.
'The Arab World': A concentrated study of its political
changes, by H. El Habtah
Baghdad: Assad Printing House, 1966**

References to Lawrence: pp 18–336.

**Abd El Kerim, A. A. et al
'The History of the Arab World: Modern Period', by
Abd El Kerim and others
Cairo: El Gimhiah Printing House**

304pp.

References to Lawrence: pp 205–14.

Hamrad, K.
'British Colonisation and the Arab World', by K. Hamrad
Cairo: National Printing House

References to Lawrence: pp 22–101, dealing with him, his relations with Philby and their influence with Abdullah El Hussein.

Maydani, Muhi el Din (trs)
'The Arabic Revolution Against the Ottoman Government', by the Director of the Army Corps in Al-Higaz, trs by Muhi el Din Maydani
Beirut: 1933

102pp, illus, 22cm

Originally published as a series of essays on the Arab Revolt in Al-Rasid.

Morris, James
'The Hashemite Kings', by James Morris
London: Faber and Faber, 1959

231pp, illus, bibl, index, 22cm.

An extremely useful history of the Hashemite Kings whose fortunes were originally linked to the British interests in the Middle East. The fortunes of the family were linked directly with the Arab Revolt and its success laid the foundation of the several Hashemite monarchies. References to Lawrence and his connections with the Hashemites are scattered throughout the book.

Mousa, Suleiman
'Hussein and the Great Arab Revolution', by Suleiman
Mousa
Amman: Printing and Distributing House, 1957

256pp, illus, maps.

Mousa, Suleiman (editor)
'Al-Thawret Al-Arabieyyeh Al-Kubra' (The Great Arab
Revolt: Documents on), edited by Suleiman Mousa
Amman: Printing and Distributing House, 1966

280pp.

This work makes no mention of Lawrence but deals with the Arab part in the Arab Revolt based on documented sources.

Mousa, Suleiman
'T. E. Lawrence: An Arab View, 1966

T. E. | LAWRENCE | AN ARAB VIEW | (rule) | Suleiman Mousa | Translated by Albert Butros | *London* | OXFORD UNIVERSITY PRESS | *New York Toronto* | 1966

x, pp (1)–301.

p (i), Half-title; verso, blank; p (iii), Title-page; verso, *Oxford University Press, Ely House, London W1* | etc | C *In English Translation Oxford University Press* 1966 | PRINTED AND BOUND IN ENGLAND BY | HAZELL WATSON AND VINEY LTD | AYLESBURY, BUCKS | ; pp (v)–vi, Contents; pp (vii)–x, Preface; pp 1–278, Text; pp (279)–287,

Comment by A. W. Lawrence and reply by Suleiman Mousa; pp (288)–90, Bibliography; pp (291)–301, Index; + 1 blank page.

This work is the first full-length study of Lawrence by an Arab and was written because of a 'sense of what one might call "cultural obligation" towards the Arab people on the one hand and the western world on the other'. Mousa felt that the writings on Lawrence and on the Arab revolt left a serious gap in information about Lawrence's life and consequently in Arab history as well. The blame for this he partially attributes to the Arab failing to put forward their side of the argument.

This work is valuable for the viewpoint which it seeks to put forward, the bibliography of Western and Arabic sources, and the analytical comment from A. W. Lawrence which appears between pp 279 and 287.

Nassar, Shaker Khalil
'Lawrence and the Arabs', by Shaker Khalil Nassar
Beirut: American Press, 1930

96pp, illus, 19cm.

An Arab view of Lawrence dealing with his early archaeological work in Asia Minor, the Arab Revolt, the peace settlement and Lawrence's life after the war.

Qadri, Dr Ahmed
'Muthakkarati' an Al-Thawret Al' Arabiyyet Al-Kubra'
(My memories of the Great Arab Revolt)
Damascus: Ibn Zaidun Press, 1956

288pp, 22cm.

This is a documented history of the Arab Revolt written by a man who was intimately concerned with the Arab nationalist movement. He was a founder member of The Arab Brotherly Society which was built on the lines of the Young Turks. He worked closely with Feisal after the war and during the Paris peace conference.

The book begins with a brief survey of Turkish rule in Arabia and goes on to discuss the growth of Arab Nationalist feeling that culminated in the foundation of the secret societies aimed at overthrowing the Turkish Empire. He then goes on to deal with the Arab Revolt and the role of Lawrence in the campaigns.

The book concludes with a section on the peace talks and the establishment of the kingdom of Syria. The author's motivation for writing his memoirs was to provide a record of the deeds of the founders of the Arabic national revival movement.

Sa'id, Amin
'The Great Arabic Revolution': A detailed history of the Arabic problem, by Amin Sa'id
Cairo: Isa al Babi al-Halabi Press, 1934

3 vols, illus, maps, bibl, index, 24cm.

vol 1, 336pp; vol 2, 130pp; vol 3, 652pp.

Contents Note:
Vol 1   The Struggle between the Arabs and Turkey.
Vol 2   The Struggle between the Arabs, the French and the English.
Vol 3   The Royalty of East Jordan, the Palestine problem, the downfall of the Hashimite government and the revolt of Al-Sham.

Salg, Anis
'The Hashimites and the Great Arabic Revolution', by
Anis Salg
Beirut: Dar Al-Talia, 1966

319pp, 24cm.

This work deals with the Hashimite leadership of the Arab revolt and the results of the revolt. It also looks at the National Movement during the revolt and the disappointment about the results of the war.

Subhi, al-Umari
'Lawrence Kama 'Araftuh' (Lawrence as I knew him)
Beirut: 1969

247pp.

Deals with Lawrence from personal experience but depends heavily on Suleiman Mousa's book *T. E. Lawrence: an Arab view* (see p 193) and *The Seven Pillars of Wisdom*. It is a critical work.

Wahba, Hafeth
'The Arab Peninsula in the Twentieth Century', by
Hafeth Wahba
Cairo: Writers Printing House, 1935

408pp, illus, maps.

References to Lawrence: pp 195-211.

Section G

Miscellaneous items

British Broadcasting Corporation
'T. E. Lawrence'
1 reel of tape (np, nd)
Tape of a broadcast made on the subject of T. E. Lawrence.
Part of the Bayard L. Kilgour Jnr collection in the Houghton
Library, Harvard University.

Cox, Sir Percy Zachariah
'Report on T. E. Lawrence's activities'
Ts, Basrah, 7 April (1916), 2s (2p).
Part of the Bayard L. Kilgour Jnr collection.

'Lawrence of Arabia memorial'
A letter of appeal to the public, signed by Allenby, Herbert
Baker, Winston Churchill, Lionel Curtis, Augustus John,
George Bernard Shaw and Evelyn Wrench, for funds to furnish
a memorial to Lawrence in St Paul's Cathedral to take the form
of the bronze head modelled by Kennington from life, with the
words 'Lawrence of Arabia' cut in the wall underneath it. Once
the memorial was paid for the committee would then consider
other forms of lasting memorial to Lawrence.

Lawrence, Thomas Edward
'Agreement between T. E. Lawrence and Jonathan Cape Ltd,
concerning the publication of *Revolt in the Desert*'
Ts (carbon copy, unsigned) London, 1925. 4s (4p). Part of the
Bayard L. Kilgour Jnr collection.

Lawrence, Thomas Edward
'A letter from T. E. Lawrence to his mother'
London: Corvinus Press, 1936
Presentation from Lord Carlow, the printer, to 'G.B.S. and
Mrs Shaw', with a long MS note by Shaw signed on endpaper.

Lawrence, Thomas Edward
Series of four letters to T. E. Willis, a friend of Lawrence whilst

he was in the Tank Corps. The letters contain personal news and are dated 5 October 1926, 26 October 1926, 3 December 1926 and 5 April 1935. These letters do not appear in David Garnett's edition of *The Letters of T. E. Lawrence* (1938) and are apparently unpublished.

These Als appear in Sotheby's sale catalogue for Tuesday, 14 December 1971 as the property of T. E. Willis Esq, and were offered for sale with Lawrence's Tank Corps cap and lapel badges which he also gave to Willis.

Lawrence, Thomas Edward
'Schneider trophy contest'
1927–9. 15 folders of material consisting of miscellaneous material and including correspondence of the Royal Aero Club, the Air Ministry, Coastal Area Headquarters and the Sea Committee. Part of the Bayard L. Kilgour Jnr collection.

Lawrence, Thomas Edward
'Seven Pillars of Wisdom'
2 AMS notebooks (np, 1925).
One notebook contains a provisional list of subscribers and other recipients of the subscribers' edition, and the other has an amplified list of recipients. An inserted sheet has a list of the final numbers, distribution, and a financial summary.

Lawrence, Thomas Edward
'Two original motion picture films of T. E. Lawrence showing trial runs of speed boats and a seaplane tender'
(Plymouth, Southampton 1932–3). Two canisters of film each 400ft long, part of the Bayard L. Kilgour Jnr collection.

———

Lawrence of Arabia (film)
Columbia Pictures: original soundtrack recording. Long-playing record.

Appendix

Notes on the writing and publication of *The Seven Pillars of Wisdom*

1919   Introduction and books 1–10 written and, according to Lawrence, all but the introduction and books 9 and 10 lost at Reading station in December 1919. The length of the text was about 250,000 words.

1920   Second text started but became very bulky (about 400,000 words). All but one page of this manuscript was destroyed by Lawrence in 1922.

1921–2   Third text drafted from the previous one with a reduction in length to 330,000 words. According to Lawrence it was composed with great care and was far superior to the 1920 text. This text was printed at the Oxford University Press; eight copies were made and four copies given to friends to read and criticise.

1926   Subscribers' edition published; a revision of the third text reduced to some 280,000 words. It has been estimated that 100 copies were sold at 30 guineas each but Lawrence maintained the figure was in excess of this though he refused to give another.

       New York Text—a proof of the subscribers' text was sent to New York and printed by Doran Publishing Co to ensure USA copyright. Only ten highly priced copies were offered for sale, with the intention of their never being sold again. Lawrence wanted no further issue of *The Seven Pillars of Wisdom* in his lifetime.

1927   Abridgement published of *The Seven Pillars of Wisdom* as *Revolt in the Desert*, containing about 130,000 words and with sufficient additions to preserve the sense and continuity. It was serialised in the *Daily Telegraph* in December 1926 and published in Britain by Cape and in the USA by Doran.

1935   First published edition of *The Seven Pillars of Wisdom* for general circulation. It has been reprinted frequently since and translated into several languages.

Index